Praise for *The Crowdsourced Performance Review*

"Eric Mosley revamps employee performance management in *The Crowdsourced Performance Review*. His book describes the importance of employee passion and happiness as the best measurement for success."

—Tony Hsieh, NY Times bestselling author of
Delivering Happiness and CEO of Zappos.com, Inc.

"Eric's book is a provocative portrait of corporate problem solving. With an engaging, fresh view of employee performance, he gives HR executives a new way to rethink appraisals. Crowdsourcing recognition is the innovation for performance management that we've been waiting for."

—Hayagreeva Rao, Atholl McBean Professor of
Organizational Behavior and Human Resources,
Graduate School of Business, Stanford University

"Eric and Globoforce have once again demonstrated why recognition is critical for today's workforce. At Symantec, we have seen firsthand how a global recognition program can unify culture and increase employee engagement. Social recognition has not only impacted our business in a positive way, it's also made HR more strategic in how we approach our most important asset, our people."

—Jennifer Reimert, Vice President of Total Rewards,
Symantec Corporation

"Crowdsourcing feedback really is an idea whose time has come. Eric clearly has a very good take on what it is to recognize people, what it is to help them to do a better job, and to use recognition to really drive higher performance in the workforce. It is a great book if you want to know how to use performance management and recognition to get more out of your workers. I would recommend it to anyone."

—John Hollon, Vice President for Editorial,
TLNT.com and ERE Media

"Eric Mosley and Globoforce have identified a significant trend impacting the future of employee performance and rewards and it's called social recognition. It's something I've seen for myself: recognition, when done well, has a profound impact on employee engagement and retention, which in turn drives business results. Eric's book is a must read for any HR leader who is seeking to capitalize on the next big transformation in employee engagement and rewards."

—Tom McMullen, Reward Practice Leader,
Hay Group North America

"Social recognition is an important new way to extend employee feedback well beyond the traditional 'manager-driven' appraisal process. Eric's book can help readers understand the principles of social recognition and the emerging role it plays in continuous performance management."

—Josh Bersin, Principal and Founder, Bersin by Deloitte, Deloitte Consulting LLP

"Don't be left behind. Read this book to find the power within the crowd to make performance management social, strategic, and meaningful. This book cuts through the performance management noise to delineate the key signal: social recognition."

—David Zinger, Global Engagement Expert and Founder of the Employee Engagement Network

"This book is a great way of thinking about a solution to a problem in talent management today. Eric is providing a new, innovative way to think about performance reviews, to think about collaboration between employees and employers. He's giving a new way to think about the workforce."

—Madeline Laurano, Research Director of Human Capital Management, Aberdeen

"Crowdsourced feedback is a new trend that HR managers and business leaders need to be thinking about. Eric's book gives managers and leaders some real ideas and insights about how they can drive recognition in their workplace; specifically, with performance reviews."

—Jessica Miller-Merrell, Chief Founder, Blogging4jobs and CEO of Xceptional HR

"This book is an excellent tool for the modern day human resources professional. It provides a framework to help HR professionals understand how social recognition can have bottom line results and also how to link it to performance management. *The Crowdsourced Performance Review* is very provocative and would be helpful for any HR professional to read."

—Laurie Ruettimann, Human Resources Consultant and Founder of Cynical Girl blog

THE
CROWD
SOURCED
PERFORMANCE
REVIEW

THE
CROWD SOURCED
PERFORMANCE REVIEW

**How to Use the Power of
Social Recognition to Transform
Employee Performance**

ERIC MOSLEY

New York Chicago San Francisco Lisbon London Madrid
Mexico City Milan New Delhi San Juan Seoul
Singapore Sydney Toronto

1 2 3 4 5 6 7 8 9 0   QFR/QFR   1 9 8 7 6 5 4 3

ISBN   978-0-07-181798-1
MHID 0-07-181798-0

e-ISBN   978-0-07-181799-8
e-MHID 0-07-181799-9

McGraw-Hill Education books are available at special quantity discounts to use as premiums and sales promotions or for use in corporate training programs. To contact a representative, please visit the Contact Us page at www.mhprofessional.com.

This book is printed on acid-free paper.

For Carol, Caoimhe, Conor, Alex, and Niamh

CONTENTS

PART 1 IMPROVING PERFORMANCE WITH THE WISDOM OF CROWDS

1 The Traditional Performance Review and the New Global Workplace   11

4 Crowdsourcing Performance with Social Recognition 69

5 The Business Case for Crowdsourcing 89

PART 2 PUTTING THE CROWDSOURCED PERFORMANCE REVIEW INTO PRACTICE

ACKNOWLEDGMENTS

A book such as this is a collaborative project built on the talents of many people. I will start by giving enormous thanks to Doug Hardy. Doug comes to a project like this with a blank page, and then proceeds to fill it with insights, creativity, patience, and hard work. Doug and I set ourselves an ambitious schedule and could not have achieved our relentless pace without the guidance and drive of Kevin Mullins.

I could not have asked for better collaborators than Derek Irvine, Charlie Ungashick, and Jessica Bergeron. Their innovation, thought leadership, and positive drive continuously propelled this project to new heights. Thanks also to Lynette Silva. Her skill as a long-term researcher has uncovered many insights over the years.

I would also like to thank the hundreds of employees of Globoforce. Their positive approach to the complexities of global culture management has made our journey possible. Globoforce is known for thought leadership, innovation, and execution on a global scale. None of this would be possible without the passion, talents, and capabilities of this incredible group of people. My heartfelt thanks to you all.

And my thanks to those incredible companies that are our clients, many of which are contributors to this book. Companies like Intuit, Fairmont Hotels & Resorts, IHG, JetBlue, and Symantec. These companies are daring, future-leaning innovators in all things culture related. It has been the highlight of my career to observe some of these great organizations and how they proactively manage their culture. They provide leadership to the rest of the business community by being passionate about recognizing and appreciating the work of their global employees. By engaging and energizing these employees, it is no surprise that they continue to be regarded as some of the best places to work. Thank you!

Introduction

The traditional performance review is frozen in time. Its design is outdated and its implementation is typically mediocre. Unless you fix it, your company itself will perform (as the review itself might say) "below expectations."

Problems with the traditional review are serious and structural. There is no quick fix. As we will see, there are culture-killing flaws embedded in the traditional review system's design. Improving execution of a broken practice won't eradicate the problems, for the pathology has already been strengthened by decades of repetition.

In theory, a performance review rewards good performance and stimulates underperforming employees to improve. This is supposed to create a cycle of ever-improving work performance based on objective criteria, raising morale and profits across the board. In practice, the traditional review often produces the *opposite* effect. Too frequently, performance reviews create discouragement, mistrust, bewilderment, cynicism, and low morale. Worse, in today's workplace, the traditional review fails to recognize and address critical changes in the way we work.

Let's consider the qualities that make the traditional review so problematic by imagining a standard performance review as it is today. It is a dull, predictable, and dreaded ritual. Employee and manager meet once a year to discuss the employee's work goals and behavior. The employee is rated on how well he or she has performed over the previous 12 months. There is a form, typically rating the employee along a numeric or phased scale ("meets expectations," "exceeds expectations," or "does not meet expectations"). It sounds something like this:

"Have a seat, Dana, and relax. I'd like to look over the last year, talk about where your work was great and where you might be able to improve. We'll go through your goals on this form and talk about expectations for the coming year.

"I especially value teamwork, Dana, and I think that's one place you really shine," says the manager. "I like the way you communicate what you're doing in our Wednesday team catch-up meeting, like last week, and I remember how you helped Ramon get up to speed with his presentations last fall. For this section, I am giving you an 'exceeds expectations' in the teamwork category."

Down the list the manager goes, and typically the talk ends with a note about money: "So, Dana, let's look forward to another good year," says the manager. "Oh, and here's the good news: we'll be raising your salary by 3.5 percent starting in January, which is above average for the company."

The ritual concluded, Dana and her manager go back to their work. Perhaps they'll chat from time to time about the goals throughout the year, but most likely, the next formal conversation focused on Dana's performance won't take place for another year, when formal performance review time rolls around again.

If this conversation sounds familiar, it's because it could have taken place in 2013, or 2003, or 1983, or even 1973! While technology, management techniques, and organizational models have undergone revolutionary change over the past few decades, the performance review has plodded along in the same format since it was invented. Even technical enhancements, such as the use of online forms, have only mimicked the old model.

Let's re imagine the performance review as it *could* appear:

"Dana," the manager begins, "this review shouldn't contain any surprises since you've been steadily getting great feedback all year. Your contributions have been recognized around the company by your peers. Here's your copy of the formal report. I'm particularly proud of the way you act on our values of teamwork and initiative. Your teamwork score is off the chart! Do you remember in April when all fifteen team members joined Ramon in giving his Teamwork award to you for making his presentations so much better? I was traveling that week but I could see the difference in his work. It's that kind of initiative that earned you the absolute maximum bonus you could get this year.

"Looking at this report, I can see you've started to have impact outside the department," he continues. "Your influence has even extended to the Paris office, given the flow of goodwill awards your contributions have earned from there."

Dana replies, "I was really gratified to see how many people agreed with the Teamwork award's sentiments. It showed how much my contribution is valued by the whole organization. The project was fun and I met a lot of people from other departments."

Like the traditional review, this new model still has structure and formality, but it has changed to include real-time, ongoing *crowdsourced* input and data. The people with whom Dana interacts have judged her performance, augmenting the single judgment of her manager. Instead of creating a one-time evaluation of performance, the manager and Dana are informed by a yearlong narrative of her accomplishments, skills, and behavior.

This crowdsourced review overcomes frustrating weaknesses of the traditional performance review using technologies and even habits that have appeared recently in the workplace.

This book reimagines the performance review system and proposes a new model, adding practices that keep pace with the extraordinary changes in business thinking and technology.

Three Innovations

Three innovations give rise to this new model:

1. The spread of crowdsourcing information of all kinds
2. The universal adoption of social media
3. The rise of culture as a competitive advantage

Here they are in somewhat more detail.

- *Crowdsourcing:* In the last decade we've seen the rise of a fascinating trend: the marriage of data from multiple sources and individual opinions to create an entirely new form of decision-making called "crowdsourcing." It's everywhere, from "star rankings" on Amazon.com's product pages to services like Angie's List, Zagat.com, and TripAdvisor. Now, people make decisions based on feedback from dozens, hundreds, or tens of thousands of other people. And these crowdsourced conclusions are replacing "expert" opinions because they are more accurate!
- *Universal social media:* In the same decade, the spread of social media has opened new channels and habits of communication. Facebook, Yammer, Yelp, LinkedIn, and other services make crowd communication a matter of (1) many people sharing information with many others in innumerable ways and (2) a new language of business.
- *Culture as competitive advantage:* For more than a decade, business thinkers have emphasized the importance of culture as a competitive advantage, as other advantages (such as factories or even patents) lose their power to confer a leading position. Influential business books from *Built to Last* to *Good to Great* make the case that an organization's culture is in fact its most important asset. Managing culture is now a central concern of both HR and C-level executives.

Social Recognition

When we bring these three innovations of crowdsourcing, social media, and culture as a competitive advantage together for the purposes of talent and culture management, the result is *social recognition*, a systematic set of practices in which many people consider and recognize an employee's performance on a daily basis.

Many of the most powerful attributes of social recognition are also seen in online star ratings. In fact, you could say that social recognition adds to performance reviews what star ratings add to online shopping. Like those critical rankings, social recognition harnesses "the wisdom of crowds" to judge performance. That is, it aggregates the opinions and thoughts of many individuals to arrive at a richer, more accurate observation of performance than one person alone could provide. The phenomenal growth of such "crowdsourced" information in the past 15 years is remaking markets and changing the way we do business.

The crowdsourced performance review adds social recognition to the traditional performance review, making it superior to the traditional review in four critical ways.

1. *It is based on data.* The new review we just previewed contains a record of specific instances in which Dana was recognized for great performance, and how it connected to company values. Even "soft" skills like leadership, innovation, and quick learning were noted.

   Data gathered about positive specific actions can provide insight into the performance of individuals, groups, and companies. These data can be generated through hundreds or thousands of "recognition moments" by tens or thousands of observers—the employees themselves as well as managers. These moments, when analyzed by the right tools, tell more about overall performance than any number of traditional review reports. With this data, managers and human resources (HR) professionals can quantify an employee's performance and progress (or lack thereof) objectively, rather than just relying on opinion.

2. *It has multiple sources of feedback.* In the traditional review, an employee is judged entirely by his or her manager. In the new format, informed opinion can be contributed by everyone with whom they come into contact, from peers to managers in different locations or departments. (In Chapter 2, we'll see how harnessing "the wisdom of crowds" gives incredible power to the new style of review.) This shared responsibility inspires the employee's trust of and engagement in the process as well as engagement in his or her job.

3. *It reviews performance in real time.* Because employees and managers are recognizing specific accomplishments throughout the year, feedback is continuous. Constant feedback is a best practice that busy managers too often let slip in the press of urgent business, but in this case, responsibility for feedback is distributed and quick. Dana's initiative in April was noted publicly and quickly, leaving a valuable trail for later review.

4. *It uses technology to make reviews more efficient.* When the traditional review was created decades ago, managing feedback about employees took months, and employees received only a snapshot of reaction once a year. Even a diligent middle manager spent an arduous week once a year filling out forms, ranking his or her employees' effectiveness, and then forgetting about the whole process for the next 51 weeks. Now, using databases and management tools, HR can respond quickly to positive and negative performance information about individuals, groups, and entire divisions of a company.

Today, a performance review system can be much more than a faster, automated replica of a 1970s paper-based process. With all the tools at your disposal, you can expect a system that matches the vast changes in business trends and technology.

Meeting that expectation requires rethinking performance management, because the traditional performance review has not kept up with the profound changes in business over the last three decades.

Chapters 1-5 of this book will explain how crowdsourcing, real-time reaction, and technology can make performance reviews more effective management tools. Chapters 6-8 will prescribe a method to merge the traditional performance review with social recognition. Chapters 9-10 will look ahead at how "big data" and the crowdsourcing phenomenon will change much more than just the performance review.

And along the way, I'll share best practices and insights that we at Globoforce have learned over the past 14 years working with our clients, many of whom are among the most admired companies in the world—companies like Intuit, InterContinental Hotels Group, JetBlue, and Symantec.

Our clients employ nearly two million employees around the world—and all are on the Globoforce platform. We've seen firsthand the challenges that HR and business leaders like you have encountered—and how they've come out more successful than ever due to the power of recognition to engage and energize employees and unify company culture.

HR is changing and transforming more dramatically than at any other time in business history. I hope you enjoy this book and share in my passion for why people are an organization's most important asset—as long as we empower them each and every day.

PART 1 IMPROVING PERFORMANCE WITH THE WISDOM OF CROWDS

1

The Traditional Performance Review and the New Global Workplace

"Liz, I'm asking for your help," said Rebecca, vice president of human resources at Hydrolab. "We are about to make some big changes in the performance review process."[1]

Liz managed product development at Hydrolab. She was a Stanford graduate who wore simple suits, studied martial arts on weekends, and listened to obscure UK garage bands. The door of the HR manager's office was closed; it was a confidential discussion.

Rebecca continued, "I checked the records of the performance review process, and you are one of the few managers who does your reviews on time, thoroughly, and thoughtfully."

Liz said evenly, "Rebecca, I like giving reviews. I've got a good team. But I'm careful about the reviews in spite of the process, not because of it."

Rebecca clicked a pen, and started to write. "What would you say is wrong with it?" she asked.

"What would you say is right with it?" asked Liz. "I'm supposed to rate 28 employees on a scale of 1 to 5 for overall performance, 1 to 5 for each job requirement, and 1 to 5 for 'potential,' whatever that is. Then on the bottom of the form I get three little lines to write comments.

"It's ridiculous to reduce something as complex as program or project management to a series of scales. For example, my department has 23 software engineers at three levels of seniority, and yet their job descriptions are more or less the same. They work at desks all day; I can't watch them, and interrupting their work is counterproductive."

The conversation continued for 30 minutes, and then Rebecca announced her plan and made her request.

"We're introducing a new performance system at a manager's meeting. We're going to unite the recognition system with the performance review system. I need your help getting the others on board."

"You want me to help get the other managers more involved in reviewing performance?" asked Liz.

"Not quite," Rebecca replied. "I want you to help get everyone at Hydrolab reviewing performance." To Liz's quizzical look, she responded, "We're going to start crowdsourcing our reviews."

Imagine someone watching apples going by on a conveyer belt. His job is to sort the apples as they go by—big, medium, small—and that goes okay as long as he can keep up. At some point, the conveyer belt speeds up a little so he has to work a little harder to keep sorting apples. The belt speeds up a bit more, and he misses a few apples as they go by. A little faster, a few more missed apples, and your worker becomes anxious.

He anticipates more speed, and more misses, and before long he's overwhelmed. Eventually, he can't possibly keep up; what does he do?

A clever apple sorter steps back from the apples and invents a grid with different sized holes that can sort the apples quickly enough to keep up. New technology, and a different way of looking at the problem, can fix the trouble that technology started.

Work information is like those apples, speeding up as technology increases the volume. Take e-mail, for example. Twenty years ago you could sort e-mail messages one at a time because you received perhaps 20 a day. You might delete a message or take action based on its information. The first step in both cases was reading the e-mail and deciding what to do with it.

But along the way the conveyor belt sped up! What used to be 20 e-mails a day became 60, and then 80, and then 100. Twitter, Facebook, Chatter, Yammer, and RSS or blog feeds joined the queue. The speed of the information conveyer belt got to an overwhelming level, and the e-mails piled up.

Information Overload

To understand the magnitude of change facing performance management, we have to start with a much bigger question facing every kind of management today: What happens when there's too much information flow? How can we sort through all those apples?

Business has moved from an information revolution to an information overload revolution. With the advent of cloud computing and mobile devices, infinite information processing power and storage capacity are available to anyone with a smartphone, and we have all become producers of unlimited streams of information in the form of e-mail, documents, conversations, tweets, and postings on social media.

Today the typical businessperson can't even keep up with the simple first step of reading the content, let alone take action. He or she might monitor as many channels of content (the aforementioned Twitter, Facebook, etc.) as individual messages 20 years ago. And rather than being self-contained messages, most of these are now streams of information that grow and multiply. Now you reply to a Facebook posting about your company's product, and you get a notification whenever someone else adds to that posting. Twitter messages multiply like hydra heads, splitting infinitely into important or trivial information streams. Interacting with all the messages individually is impossible.

This is the information overload condition. The information overload revolution consists of ways in which business learns how to manage the condition, and even takes advantage of the endless stream of information, to separate the valuable from the worthless, and leverage the most important information from customers, employees, stockholders, and all the others in a business's universe of stakeholders.

Search-Led Information Processing

As we move from finite storage (physical files and disk space) to infinite storage (databases and clouds), we shift our focus from storing information to retrieving it. Rather than carefully filing valuable information up front, we now build better ways to search all of our information for valuable content.

Finite storage meant making choices about what to save. In years past, I'd get an e-mail from Bob, and I'd put it in the "Bob" folder. Mary's e-mails went into the "Mary" folder, or because she works in finance, I might have put her e-mails in the "Finance" folder.

I gave up filing e-mails five years ago. Now I have a single storage folder for e-mails, and I've switched from filing to searching that folder. I no longer design a filing scheme in advance. That used to take a lot of time, and it was quickly outdated. The emphasis has changed from dealing with information immediately and comprehensively to dealing with information when I need it, from up-front filing to future retrieval.

This dynamic scales with the amount of data. In fact, the advent of search engine optimization (SEO) and its methods, such as tagging of all content, is an Internet-wide version of the same practice. This works with content channels as well as e-mail. Except for a few favorite sources, I don't rely on websites for the business news I need (analogous to going to a file called "business news"); I use a custom Google search so that information relevant to my business is continuously delivered to me.

The move from filing to searching is a fundamental shift. It's novel to older generations, but millennial workers have grown up in this continuous stream of information, and their work habits reflect their comfort with it. Their experience points to the inexorable evolution from filing to search.

Move from Synchronous to Asynchronous Search

Moving from filing to search also changes information work from synchronous to asynchronous. Synchronous refers to work tasks that occur together; for example, you complete a task and move on to the next task. Mail came to the in-box, it got processed, and responses went into the out-box. Asynchronous means work without the use of fixed time intervals; for example, you partially complete a task, you move on to another task, you move back. When I'm working on a task, a search of my computer will retrieve all relevant e-mails, documents, web pages, and blog messages I saved on that topic today, yesterday, and two years ago. My information work is not bound by time or sequence of tasks.

The search model relieves an individual from the need to create endless information trees, rubrics, and the like for managing his or her information. If you're following three people on Twitter, you might feel obligated to read everything they post. If you're following 500 people, the idea of reading everything is absurd; you have already crossed over to the place where automation is the only answer to finding the right information. You might step into the stream from time to time for the pleasure or creative inspiration of serendipity, just as you will probably continue to scan highly focused information sources, such as the website of the Society of Human Resources Management (SHRM). But for general purposes, the model of automating the retrieval of important information, to evolve from sorting apples by hand to building an apple-sorting machine, is the efficient and inevitable model.

These capabilities are potentially great tools for human resources planning and performance management, as we shall see. In the social recognition model, the manager allows the employee base (the crowd) to rate and review the employees throughout the year through positive feedback, building data and connections that can be reviewed (searched) asynchronously. With the speed of change in business, human resources can use all the help it can get.

It's Twitter's World

The millennial generation consumes information differently from all its predecessors, illustrated by the astonishing rise of Twitter. A few years ago, Twitter seemed trivial to businesses, which typified it by mocking its content like, "Hey, I'm eating a sandwich!" Twitter was quickly adopted by the digital elite as a reporting-in-real-time platform, memorably at the 2007 South by Southwest (SXSW) digital media conference, and by 2009 it burned into world consciousness as the frontline reporting medium in the Iranian presidential election protests. Today, hundreds of millions of people use Twitter's 140-character messaging format to spread information and awareness via weblinks, hashtags, retweets, and Twitter's other conventions.

This is a different form of communication from newspapers, radio, television, or even websites. Twitter is a continuous stream of content from many sources gathering around a subject, whether it's history in the making (the Arab Spring) entertainment (Academy Award nominations), gossip (Hollywood pregnancies), or news (live reports from a political convention). Twitter users can create a customized collection of the content they will view as it appears, or even follow "what's trending on Twitter" to simply check in on what is popular, that is, viewed and shared, among the millions of daily tweets.

Consuming this news is different from reading or listening to or watching a story following the classic journalistic "inverted pyramid" of a beginning, middle, and end. It is a different experience from reading an essay or listening to a story. In Twitter's world, the consumer captures and filters information from many sources, often in an asynchronous manner—a stream of text, pictures, video, and audio information.

There are similar applications used by websites to add meaning to single stories, for example, the constantly updated box of "most e-mailed stories" at *The New York Times* website or "most watched videos" at YouTube. In both cases it's the crowd of users that determines the standing of an item on the list. The more popular a story or video at the moment, the higher it climbs.

What's important to note about this "Twitterfying" of information is that it is a *nonlinear, crowd-resourced, crowd-filtered,* and *self-edited* experience. Information is published by the crowd, filtered by the crowd, and consumed by individuals to whom the crowd is a reliable standard of significance for any given information.

Technology tends to create physical and emotional habits (prime example: if you don't get an answer to a search engine query in less than three seconds, you wonder what's wrong, and reload the query). These habits are both acquired and unconscious. As people find value in the new model of streaming and use it more, streaming becomes the majority's way of accessing and acquiring information.

Habits are also not built on randomness; in fact, predictability is the reason to acquire a habit, and so the mind that consumes information in a stream rather than single packets is working hard to recognize patterns, reinforce prejudices, challenge assumptions, or whatever the individual intends. And as it is with the mind, it is with the software that organizes and publishes a stream of content. Pandora's Beatles playlist isn't random—it's based on what the crowd thinks of individual Beatles songs (and based on what individuals whose tastes are similar to yours listen to on Pandora—what songs they choose, when they listen, how long they listen, etc.).

Can all these opinions, put together, actually render an accurate picture of the world? As we see in the next chapter, it is not only possible but, under the right conditions, collating and averaging opinions can render a more accurate picture than relying on "expert" opinion.

The Young Want It All—and They're Right

Since the beginning of time, bosses have grumbled, "Kids these days want it all." They mean by this that younger workers want to do things their own way. No more eight-year apprenticeships making the coffee and doing the lower-end work. Those who manage the millennial generation (people who were born after 1980) say the same, of course, but they risk missing differences that amount to more than youthful impatience.

First, in the modern organization, the lower-end work is gone. Technology does the copying, collating, and mailing. The boss makes his or her own coffee fresh at the Keurig machine. Nobody sends a fax. The cleaning service and phone maintenance are outsourced to another company. Young people entering the company in white-collar jobs have to be more skilled, motivated, and fast-moving than their predecessors because that's the only way they'll get a decent business job (not to mention a decent job in public service, teaching, etc.—but for simplicity's sake let's stick with the office work model).

Second, millennials are not blindly loyal to a company. Why should they be? Their parents were loyal and got laid off in every recession. They are not actively disloyal, however. They see work as a contract, an understanding that they'll contribute work as long as their needs are met. They are also more loyal to teammates and colleagues than to bosses and companies.

They also need more than a paycheck. Since they know that job security is a thing of the past and that they will probably work for a dozen companies in the first 20 years of their careers, they seek more than security.

Beyond the paycheck, millennials want their work to mean something—to fulfill a mission, to create great products, to serve customers, to accomplish personal expectations of excellence, or excitement, or travel, or experience. To be recognized.

Beyond Work/Life Balance

Those employees known as millennials (also called gen Y) are changing the work/life balance discussion forever. Millennials are not as concerned with balancing their work life and their personal life because they often do not clearly differentiate between the two. Work and personal time are so blended for them that relationships at work and the ability to work anytime, anywhere are important aspects of their day. For this and other reasons, millennials especially are seeking purpose and meaning in their work. A powerfully positive way to give them this purpose and meaning is by incorporating your company values into a recognition program. This gives millennials a sense of purpose and accomplishment within the bigger picture while also emphasizing the importance of living the company values in their daily work.

Fortunately, a company that can provide these opportunities for millennials will have the pick of the litter because this generation's mobility inclines its members to go where the greatest amount of satisfaction can be gained, whether they want money or prestige or personal pride in a job well done—or all of these and more.

Third, there are substantial differences in the experience and talents of this generation of tech-savvy, media-soaked employees. They were using personal computers by age six. They were interacting with complex virtual worlds by age eight (video games like *The Sims*). They do not remember a time without the web, e-mail, instant messaging, and 300-channel cable television. And they build and maintain relationships both the old-fashioned way—at school, playing sports, going to church—and the virtual way, on social media sites like Facebook. They learn, date, play, and do business online. Skype and smartphones make their sense of time and distance more flexible than that of their elders.

Premillennial generations were brought up to complete each task at work including working with information. "You've got to finish the task,"

Research Insight

Millennials Leading the Way

"Collective intelligence, crowd-sourcing, smart mobs, and the 'global brain' are some of the descriptive phrases tied to humans working together to accomplish things in a collaborative manner online. Internet researcher and software designer Fred Stutzman said the future is bright for people who take advantage of their ability to work cooperatively through networked communication. 'The sharing, tweeting, and status updating of today are preparing us for a future of ad hoc, always-on collaboration,' he wrote. 'The skills being honed on social networks today will be critical tomorrow, as work will be dominated by fast-moving, geographically diverse, free-agent teams of workers connected via socially mediating technologies.'"[2]

—Janna Quitney Anderson and Lee Rainie,
Pew Research Center's Internet & American
Life Project, 2012

they were told. "Don't start something that you don't finish." "Finish your dinner." Finishing, that is, using up every possible resource before moving on to fresh resources, became a work habit, too.

In an overload situation, the first thing you have to accept is that you can't finish every task that appears. You have to prioritize. Let's take a lesson from many millennials who have grown up in this environment: They are often selective about which tasks are finite and must be finished and which are ongoing processes. In a world of unlimited information, following and generating information are decidedly the latter. For them, reading all the e-mails and information channels is not the point; getting to the right information quickly is the point.

People who have mastered this new work milieu participate in the stream as both creators and consumers of information. And that brings us to the good news for performance management, because their new habits make a better performance review possible.

The Work Stream

The workplace is a continuous flow of conversation, e-mail, tasks, events, teamwork, individual work, urgent and trivial tasks—the life of work. Everyone who is even barely alert participates in this flow. People work together and observe others working in the next cubicle or loading dock, forming relationships and opinions while writing the story of their work lives in their minds.

What is less obvious and very new is that these moments can be captured and recorded discretely to create a picture of work taking place as it happens. The importance of this can hardly be overstated, because if you record, encourage, and replicate the way work is approached by individuals, you can direct that behavior toward better outcomes.

In past decades, this is what management consultants did when they observed behaviors and the results of those behaviors. They then presented executives with a 50-slide PowerPoint deck called "best practices." They were gathering information about which behaviors achieved results and which behaviors didn't. They studied team dynamics, which is an anthropological way of saying that they studied how people work together and, crucially, how they act on what they observe in others.

W. Edwards Deming's grasp of workplaces as social systems as well as productive systems led to the quality revolution of the 1970s and 1980s. He first demonstrated his ideas in Japan, and the increasing quality of inexpensive Japanese goods cost U.S. manufacturers enormous market share in automobiles, electronics, and other industries. Now Deming's concepts are commonplace. Yet the improvement of the social systems of work was complicated enough that business process analysis remained the exclusive work of management consultancies, or organizational experts, until recently.

Today, that research work of management consultants can be outsourced to the people who do the work. The day-to-day reality of the work stream and people's willingness to record the stream appropriately creates the conditions necessary for a system to find best practices on a continuous basis.

Information management software is the enabling technology. Here's a popular example: Some modern e-mail systems "learn" how you use e-mail and adjust the priorities of messages according to your behavior over time. If you always reply to Cynthia's e-mails, the system presents them more prominently than other, less-important messages. The system learns over time to distinguish, in the popular phrase, signal (information you want) from noise (information you don't want, or at least want less urgently).

Twitter and the rest have habituated employees to continuously notice and record bits of reality around themselves. Most of the time they don't need motivation, just tools. Add a little motivation, and the stream really starts to flow.

If the stream is composed of the right information; if it is searchable; if it is designed to reflect the values of a healthy company culture; if everyone uses it, the stream yields actionable information about individual performance. This *crowdsourced* information captures performance information as it occurs and when it occurs, and it is filtered by the people best able to affirm its relevance—the workforce itself.

Human Resources Overwhelmed

All management practices today struggle to keep up with the pace of this information overload. The information stream means that one by one hidden competitive advantages fall and competitive pressures mount. Speed to market, customization, innovation, global competitors, low barriers to imitation and entry have created relentless pressure to become both more productive and more efficient.

Today, vital customer insight is available instantly. Customer feedback about every product and service is published across the web and produced in custom forms for businesses seeking to improve their products and understand their customers. Huge quantities of data on every interaction with customers, vendors, and fellow employees are generated every day (interoffice e-mail is just the tip of the iceberg).

This is information that the last generation's business thinkers could hardly imagine. Database analytic software extracts meaningful facts from these data, shedding light on everything from what color of bathrobe customers in Pennsylvania prefer to how quickly employees can fill out an expense report.

Against these changes, HR has lagged in the sense that companies don't capture much information about actual behaviors among employees. While it's possible to log the flow of e-mail, or productive output, not that much is recorded or understood about how people interact. This is especially true in the area of judging and improving the performance of those complicated and critical assets we call "human beings." Data on individual performance are subjective and sparse. People are pigeonholed into files with labels like "high potential," "average," or "technical." Even more sophisticated practices, like temperament analysis or balancing team performance, are based on the notion that work goes best when you nail down a few essential facts about people, put them in the file, and watch them perform.

The performance review, as we see below, is the sad poster child of this outdated view. Deciding how a person performs is a fine and necessary discipline, but it is based on prearranged, static "files" called job descriptions, expectations, and deliverables that are decided entirely in advance.

What if performance assessments instead were based on a continuous stream of information? What if, at any time, a large database of factual information about a workforce's performance, as individuals and as a group, could be searched according to the need at hand? Instead of deciding in advance how a high-performing group should be constructed, what if an HR manager could monitor the actions of any group against its performance goals to discover what is currently unknown but important?

Before we examine how to bring these changes to performance management, let's see once and for all where today's traditional performance review is broken.

What if performance assessments were based on a continuous stream of information?

The Troubled Traditional Performance Review

The flaws inherent in the traditional review can be fixed. It's not necessary to scrap the system entirely. Traditional reviews fulfill significant functions in the context of the business at large.

As we reimagine the performance review, it's beneficial to consider the current system's *positive* contributions:

- *Legal compliance:* Businesses are subject to legal requirements in hiring, assessing, and firing employees. Performance systems leave an audit trail documenting the company's interactions with an individual.
- *Manager guidance:* Managers need to start *somewhere*. Because few managers receive formal training in preparing reviews, the tradi-

"The traditional performance review renders an accurate description of the quality of the workforce."

A Globoforce/Society for Human Resource Management survey asked, "Do you think the annual performance reviews are an accurate appraisal for employees' work?"

Only 55% of HR professionals answered "yes."

MYTHBUSTER

tional review supplies at least a template for telling employees what's expected of them and how they're doing. (This is positive only in the sense that it's something rather than nothing.)

- *The need to differentiate:* Not everyone deserves a trophy. A culture that doesn't recognize and reward engagement and high performance will not have engaged high performers for long. Keeping people in place who aren't performing is not good for them or the organization. And those who need to improve should be identified, coached, and motivated.

- *The need to advance:* The specific categories of skills used by traditional reviews can point high-potential employees toward acquiring more of the right skills they would need for advancement. This facilitates strong career paths, grooms future leadership, and aids succession planning.

- *The need to be inclusive:* There are a few jobs so specialized, or so isolated from the company at large, that a fair assessment can be made only by an expert individual with respect to very specific goals and behaviors. (Imagine a statistical analyst or software engineer working alone from home.) The traditional review template cannot accommodate these jobs.

- *The need to encourage performance management:* The traditional review grew in reaction to a situation in which every manager judged employees by gut feel (or predisposition or whim). That just exaggerates the "single point of failure" problem. For all its flaws, the traditional review enforces a process in which employees and managers must discuss performance. Put in the weakest terms, it's better than nothing.

- *The need to measure something:* Although its data are flawed, the traditional review can potentially render insights into employee strengths and weaknesses as a whole and can connect employee performance with overall financial performance. HR is routinely confronted with the need to quantify its claims, and yet the profession has been chronically weak in proving its worth with hard data. The traditional review offers some data.

The traditional performance review has been around for decades, and its presence owes a lot to inertia. Managers and HR staff are familiar with it, trained in its methods, and able to use it to manage performance however imperfectly. The traditional review is not the best conceivable system, but it is a set of habits understood by everyone and is likely to be around for a long time.

Bearing its contributions in mind, let's examine the flaws that dilute the power of traditional reviews to manage individual performance and contribute to a larger performance culture. Traditional performance reviews:

- Bear a single point of potential failure
- Limit their own scope by locking down in advance the work behaviors to be discussed over the year
- Are structurally limited to a narrow range of information
- Are only tenuously objective
- Observe only a small set of employee behaviors
- Are difficult to scale across a large organization
- Do not inspire employee engagement

At the end of this chapter, I also consider two inadvertent drawbacks of today's traditional review: Its flaws are enabled and even magnified by many current technologies, and it is subject to extreme interpretations that defeat the very purpose for which it was designed.

A Single Point of Failure

Traditional performance reviews are typically written by one manager, based on the insights and observations of that manager, and conducted by that manager. This makes that one manager a potential single point of failure for the process. As the sole gatekeeper of the review process, he or she must be an impartial expert in ranking performance, an effective coach, and an excellent communicator, all at once. How many managers fit that description?

The documenting of the manager's opinion becomes hugely important to each employee because the employee's career and reputation is built upon the manager's opinion. Over time, that reputation is encased in a sequence of official performance reviews, each conducted by a single individual. If a review is inaccurate or poorly done—or prejudiced—the reputation becomes a long documented series of misleading opinions.

Negative reviews engender a "doom loop" for an employee's reputation: they lead to low expectations and limited opportunities. These in turn feed all sorts of career-limiting consequences such as being passed over for promotion, lower compensation, and the crushing awareness of being labeled inferior. Unless intervention successfully breaks the cycle, failure becomes a self-fulfilling prophecy, and employee failure means a loss of the investment—including recruiting, training, and management time—the company has put into that employee.

Are negative reviews always unjustified? Not at all, but the single point of failure is a structural defect that endangers the entire performance management process.

In comparison, consider the consequences of an overly positive review. Imagine someone who is an average performer but an excellent office politician. The manager's favorite, he or she showcases work, navigates egos and bureaucratic red tape, and flatters and promotes the boss's interests. Is it possible that this person might receive rewards greater than his or her contribution merits? Might people who are more productive but less skilled in communicating their value notice and resent this situation? Is the best performance receiving the best reward? The answer is obvious to experienced HR staff: We've all known such people!

These commonplace scenarios sow cynicism, mistrust, and low morale among employees. Is this the way to build a stronger workforce?

Managers promoted up through the ranks have often arrived in their position because they are skilled in their field. An expert software engineer or accountant or project manager might lack management skills, especially skills he or she has never been required to use. How are they supposed to be good at reviewing performance? They rarely receive training, participate in a standardized system, or even get coaching from a more experienced manager. Practice is infrequent, so real expertise is hard to acquire.

The skills that make a good reviewer, coach, or mentor are not always present in managers who have risen to their position for a variety of accomplishments. For example, a manager might not possess the communication skills appropriate to providing critical feedback to constructive effect. In a formal, structured setting, many managers feel unduly constrained by the forms and format of a traditional review. Moreover, some managers simply lack insight, empathy, or understanding outside their technical areas of expertise.

Annually or semiannually, these managers consider the performance of each team member, rank those individuals as best they can, and then return to the daily complexities of management. The real practice of assessing and appropriately rewarding performance is an afterthought for many. Furthermore, managers are not omniscient; they cannot spend a work year trying to observe every staffer at all times, taking meticulous notes all the while.

Managerial temperament bends the system, too. In a 2010 Worldat-Work/Sibson study, 63 percent of respondents felt that managers' lack of courage to have difficult performance discussions was the top challenge in performance management. Employees felt that feedback was inconsistent and not provided in a timely manner. (If management were easy, business bestseller lists wouldn't cycle a seemingly endless supply of management advice.[3])

In response to the single point of failure problem, HR invests in automated or standardized systems of performance management and coaches and cajoles managers to improve the accuracy of their performance management. Sometimes HR introduces more complicated techniques, like 360-degree reviewing (more on that below). HR makes the best of a flawed setup.

The annual review is outdated in the world of the work stream. It is a static statement in time. Typically, managers' judgments about performance that will color the next 365 days are based on reactions to the last 365 days. Talk about a file-bound system!

A Narrow Range of Information

Even if performance review systems compensated for managerial lack of expertise, structural flaws in the traditional review narrow the range of information it provides compared to the range of behaviors it attempts to review. It is not timely. It does not provide enough actionable data to executive management for the purpose of strategic workforce assessment and planning. As it is now structured, the traditional review contains internal contradictions, is too subjective, and is too limited in the behaviors it addresses.

In the annual or semiannual performance review routine, executives receive only a broad assessment of the company's workforce quality, taken at a single point in time. Even if the assessment were 100 percent accurate (unlikely), what would sustain current performance? How might it be improved? Who in the workforce is truly engaged in his or her work? Whose work affirms the strategy and values of the company, and who is off-track? Who might be performing brilliantly but not receiving encouragement, recognition, and reward? Which managers are producing great performance because of their great management, and which are just lucky? What data do performance assessment systems provide, and how might the data be used to improve a company's financial or mission performance?

Most traditional review systems cannot accurately answer these questions, even though the answers would unlock hidden potential throughout the organization.

A Flawed Rewards Structure

The traditional review has vivid structural flaws with respect to decisions concerning who gets the money. In theory, a manager is given a specified amount of money to distribute in the form of raises and performance bonuses and then allocates more for high performers and less for low performers. If managers were both skilled and impartial, that structure might be fair, or at least transparent, but studies show that managers are inconsistent in their assessments and rewards.

Perversely, managers are often encouraged to downplay the connection between the performance review and an annual salary change. This is supposed to legitimize the review as a tool for personal growth, but in practice everyone knows that the review and the raise are bound together. If they weren't, the concept of "merit pay" would be a logical fallacy, and employees would have no monetary incentive to improve.

Metrics-based reward systems, such as sales commissions, are more transparent, but advancement in sales organizations still requires the subjective judgments of a review. Earning a high commission or bonus does not necessarily testify to an employee's leadership qualities, strategic insight, or ability to manage others.

> *Earning a high commission or bonus does not necessarily testify to an employee's leadership qualities, strategic insight, or ability to manage others.*

The "Objective" Illusion

The most corrosive contradiction of the traditional review is that it is intended to be an objective performance assessment, but its execution is subjective, relying on broad judgment calls from managers. Although performance review instruments attempt to measure actions objectively, employees know that their reputation lies with the manager's opinion, not the data.

The traditional review emphasizes the power imbalance between employee and manager. Managers are empowered to rank employees' work, but the employees have no power either to rank their own performance or to rank their manager's performance. This naturally raises the question of managerial objectivity. Is a manager giving good ratings just to employees he or she likes? Former GE CEO Jack Welch addressed this pitfall in typically blunt fashion in his book *Winning:*

It is true, without question, that at some companies, differentiation is corrupted by cronyism and favoritism. The top 20 percent are the boss's head-nodders and buddies, and the bottom 10 percent are the outspoken types who ask difficult questions and challenge the status quo. The middle 70 are just ducking and getting by. That happens and it stinks, and it is a function of a leadership team lacking in brains or integrity or both.

The only good thing I can say about a merit-free system like this is that eventually it destroys itself.[4]

Some models, such as 360-degree review, in which selected peers, executives, and staff members all contribute to a manager's review, attempt to address the question of subjectivity by adding a few other voices to the system. They constitute a small minority of total reviews and have their own contradictions.[5] For example, the social politics of the 360-degree review encourage a complex set of alliances, rivalries, and log-rolling among peers.

In practice, 360-degree reviews can actually muddy the waters. According to an authoritative 2012 study "A serious problem for multi-source appraisals is that they often present the employee with conflicting messages about his or her performance . . . This problem becomes much more serious when decisions about promotions or raises are dependent on . . . the employee's subsequent performance improvement."[6]

The result? In the 360-degree environment the input is watered down to the point where it becomes generic. Whenever people have to give an opinion, they become diplomatic in their responses. Candor and thus accuracy are lost.

Another pitfall: Individual managers have different degrees of confidence in the traditional performance review as a management tool. One might spend five hours preparing each review and another hour with each employee, earnestly trying to get the most out of the system. Another might spend ten minutes filling out a form with "gut calls" and then deliver the feedback to the employee and executive management with an off-the-cuff "I know what my people need and who my winners and losers are."

Objectivity is not necessarily an ideal state. Everyone forms opinions based on values, goals, outcomes, perceived effort, and performance. Organizational behavior is complex and subject to forces within and outside each individual's control. Few jobs can be judged on purely objective criteria, so it's appropriate that opinion come into play. But the complexity of most jobs creates yet another problem.

Traditional Performance Reviews Observe Only a Small Set of Behaviors

Traditional performance review structure reflects an outdated paradigm of work: Jobs and performance are completely quantifiable in advance. Work has changed.

On an old-fashioned assembly line, a manager could measure how many steering columns a person produced in one hour. That was a one-dimensional measurement, disconnected from the production process, the quality of the work, or the appeal of the finished product. (A broader focus on process, quality, and design helped Japan's automakers overwhelm Detroit in the 1980s and 1990s.)

Those days are long gone. Even entry-level jobs today are complex, nuanced, and unpredictable. They require hard-to-quantify attributes like problem solving, teamwork, creativity, and adaptability to change.

Can "initiative" or "teamwork" be quantified? Managers *try* to quantify these qualities by remembering specific instances in which the employee demonstrated them. Employees are encouraged to come to a performance review with examples of times they exhibited problem solving or good teamwork. Anecdotal evidence helps (at least it jogs a manager's memory), but it prejudices reviews in favor of the good communicators. If you follow this scenario to its logical conclusion, then employees get a good review if they're good at playing the review system in their favor. What does that have to do with actual performance? (This is similar to a problem known to recruiters everywhere: The job doesn't always go to the strongest performer, but to the person who is strongest in presenting his or her candidacy.)

The system needs a better method than relying solely on manager-employee dialogue. The missing players in the traditional performance review process are everyone else who comes in contact with the employee.

The Traditional Review Is Difficult to Scale

In practice, most traditional review tools and approaches suffer from underuse. Managers don't take the time to create discrete goals for each individual. The effort sounds wonderful in theory, but in practice you just can't get busy people to take on the administrative overhead. Say you have 20,000 people in your company, with the average manager responsible for writing 20 reviews. That creates 1,000 "bookkeepers" logging the progress of their employees, and that process, dependent on each bookkeeper, doesn't scale well.

Each of those manager-bookkeepers has to be trained in the art of reviewing well, and their expertise should be monitored. In practice, this is a huge task for human resources, and unfortunately, it's a secondary concern for most, both inside and outside HR.

Traditional Reviews Do Not Inspire Engagement

Employee engagement is a burning priority for employers because workers who give extra effort voluntarily boost productivity, profits, and competitive advantage at no extra cost. While the traditional review can sometimes *recognize* engagement, it's a poor instrument for *inspiring* engagement.

Engagement, energy, and urgency—you see these qualities in behaviors, not because the goals were written on a form in January but because they are experienced day by day.

Imagine an employee who works in the marketing department. We'll call him Kevin. It's late in the evening on August 31, and Kevin is the last one in the office. He's late to get away for a three-day weekend, but as

"Our employees trust the system because it's objective and the same for everyone."

Does a standardized performance review system inspire trust? In a 2010 survey of HR professionals by WorldatWork/Sibson Consulting, only 30 percent of respondents reported their employees trust the performance management system!

MYTH**BUSTER**

he prepares to leave, he hears the phone ring and sees on the display that it's a client. He can choose to answer it, with the possible consequence of having to stay at work even later, or he can leave and nobody will know.

Kevin answers the phone and, since he understands the product in question, stays on the line for 90 minutes, helping the customer solve a problem.

What makes him pick up the phone? Character, yes, but Kevin's behavior also reflects a company culture that consistently says, "We go out of our way to help customers, no matter what." Kevin goes out of his way because he's engaged in his job in ways that reflect company values. Culture delivers that extra piece of performance that makes him stay. Self-motivated service is one of the behavioral norms of Kevin's workplace. If he worked in a dysfunctional company where the culture involved politicking and disrespect for customers, it would be a badge of honor to not answer the phone and just leave.

Back in January, Kevin's manager did not say, "Now, Kevin, some day a customer is going to call late in the evening. I want you to pick up the phone and help that customer, even if nobody is around to notice." It's not even in Kevin's job description to help a customer with the product. This is not a "deliverable" or a "goal" or a set behavior on a form, but an attitude. That attitude is embedded in the company's culture. Kevin understands the culture, and this makes Kevin able to do the right thing in unanticipated situations.

Many traditional review processes try to address this positive situation in advance by talking about company values, but by its nature an annual review can do so only in a generic way. As a result of not knowing all the different things Kevin might need to do, his manager has to be generic in Kevin's job description. While terms like "customer-centric" and "dedicated" are better than nothing, the traditional review is not structured to recognize, record, or quantify the engagement Kevin showed. He has a voluntary mindset and improvises appropriate solutions in all kinds of different situations.

Ultimately, a healthy culture of engagement based on company values is what a strong performance system should reinforce.

Research Insight

"The key to driving productivity gains is increasing engagement among core contributors, who represent 60 percent of the typical workforce. Highly engaged employees are already working at or near their peak but are often limited by their less engaged coworkers. Focusing on engaging core contributors can improve both groups' productivity."

—Watson Wyatt Worldwide, 2008/2009
WorkUSA Report

The Trouble with Technology

Performance management technology as it is currently deployed was designed to automate traditional HR processes, with the result being that it has perpetuated flaws that existed in the old paper-based approach. It's easier to aggregate data from 1,000 web-based forms than 1,000 paper forms, but that doesn't address the underlying flaws in the system.

Other innovations in performance technology might compensate for managers' weaknesses yet inadvertently create new problems. For example, there's a SaaS (Software-as-a-Service) technology that supplies simple drag-and-drop text for managers to report performance. If a manager wants to say that Susan showed innovation in her job, he or she doesn't have to tell a story or even think very hard: The manager just drops in the "innovative" text. So now the system has dumbed down the human observation of Susan's behavior. Everybody who has shown the spirit of innovation has the same text describing his or her performance. Instead of increasing differentiation among human performers, the system has encouraged generic reviews that don't describe the differences between employees.

Some performance management technology tools are capable of describing goals more flexibly. Here the problem is their low level of adoption among managers. Managers skip over the step, returning to generic descriptions because in the spectrum of modern jobs, goals don't naturally flow down into a company in a beautiful waterfall effect.

Stack Ranking: Reviewing at the Extreme

To magnify the shortcomings of the traditional review, let's take a look at its exaggerated variant, called "stack ranking," which is a formula-driven form of differentiation. Broadly, stack ranking forces managers to categorize a small percentage of employees as top players, a large percentage as average, and a small percentage as underperforming. All managers must rank their groups according to this formula. An outstanding group gets the same percentage of top players as a group that is only so-so or worse.

"Uniformity of reviews guarantees accuracy and fairness."

One-size-fits-all performance review systems are created for the convenience of administration, not for fairness or quality data. You don't have uniform objectives, job descriptions, feedback, or working conditions across the organization. How can a single performance review system render an accurate picture?

MYTHBUSTER

Stack ranking and its variants are extreme examples of how the need to assess and improve employee performance can be hopelessly misdirected. A structured, inflexible, top-down model, goes the theory, will create effective ranking, selecting the best and weeding out the worst.

More than anyone, Jack Welch, the former CEO of GE, was responsible for the popularity of differentiation, but its practitioners have often strayed from Welch's rigorous implementation principles such as candor, careful coaching, and transparency. Yes, Welch insisted on differentiating employees by performance into top 20 percent, middle 70 percent, and bottom 10 percent, and then showering rewards on the top, coaching the middle, and getting rid of the bottom. Actually carrying out such a structure to positive effect is extremely difficult. It took GE more than ten years to establish enough candor in its managers and trust in its rank-and-file for the system to become effective.

About the majority of employees, Welch wrote, "The middle 70 percent . . . is enormously valuable to any company; you simply cannot function without their skills, energy, and commitment. . . .

And that's the major challenge, and risk, in 20-70-10—keeping the middle 70 engaged and motivated. . . . *Everyone* in the middle 70 needs to be motivated and made to feel as if they truly belong."[7]

An example of how stack ranking can be misused was cited in the August 2012 *Vanity Fair*. The article, "How Microsoft Lost Its Mojo," traced the trials of the software company from 1999, when its stock price hit an all-time high, to 2012. The article blamed Microsoft's missteps, lost opportunities, and lack of innovation on a suffocating bureaucracy with stack ranking driving all sorts of poor choices.[8]

The article listed many pernicious effects of misinterpreting Jack Welch's theory. Reviews based on a bell-curve model caused people to game the system in ways unrelated to performance. Employees competed with each other for management attention and approval. It was better to be a strong performer on a weak team than to be a strong performer on a strong team. Employees' attention focused on competing with each other for dollars, rather than beating other software companies. Short-term thinking became habitual.

Stack ranking was intended to end an earlier performance review problem: grade inflation. In the past, managers would give almost everyone on their team an average ranking of 4 out of 5. They never managed a 2, and very rarely a 5. Who wants to lead a team of underachievers? A big company might have 80 percent of employees with a 4 rating and no systematic way to identify and nurture high-potential talent.

In practice, stack ranking perpetuates the very problem it was intended to fix and adds a host of unintended, negative consequences. It is an inflexible system intended to manage the very fluid, changing interactions of unpredictable business events and complex, multitalented people.

Stack ranking is just like the traditional review, but more extreme.

Can This System Be Saved?

The traditional review's flaws can be fixed. Its single point of failure can be supplemented by additional inputs if done correctly. A better performance review system will:

- Remediate the "single point of failure" threat inherent in today's manager-centric system
- Preserve the manager's accountability for performance
- Set performance objectives that adapt to changing business conditions and include unanticipated deliverables that go above and beyond the job description
- Recognize the importance of employee engagement and company culture
- Assess employee performance from many sources—the peers, managers, internal customers, and others who witness day-to-day work, supplying much more data via *crowdsourced* information from the front lines of business
- Observe hard-to-quantify factors like creativity and self-discipline
- Render detailed analyses of performance on a host of individual, group, and companywide factors and relate them directly to overall performance metrics such as revenue, profit, and time-to-market
- Maintain the strengths of the traditional performance review

Social recognition, in which employees award each other for observed great performance, alleviates the shortcomings of the traditional review. It is not a complete or radical substitute. The traditional review is established, and as we have seen, it has some useful qualities. What is needed is a balance of traditional review and social recognition inputs in a larger, ongoing, day-to-day system of performance management. Combine the formal, scheduled, one-to-one process of traditional reviews with the informal, spontaneous, many-to-many capabilities of social recognition, and a modern, robust performance management system comes into being.

All of social recognition's capabilities are based on the new source of information that drives the global movements discussed at the beginning of this chapter. To understand how a continuous stream of information feeds performance management, it is necessary to dive into the practice of gathering and analyzing information from many sources in a meaningful way. Dealing with information overload proactively is the next phase of the information revolution.

2 Crowdsourcing and Human Resources

Rebecca was good at getting managers fired up, stalking the stage, and liberally enlisting comments from Hydrolab's CEO Trevor, who sat in the front row.

The change Hydrolab introduced today would need some explaining. To focus the minds of the skeptical, Rebecca decided to go straight to two gut issues—money and power.

"This year we're starting a new performance review process. I think it will interest you because the bottom line is this: You will have more power and money to reward performance in 2013." She let this sink in, and then continued.

"How will you have more power? By giving it away!"

Confused looks. Trevor kept a serene smile. Rebecca moved to the next slide showing a simple drawing of a network.

"You engineering managers say the power of a network grows exponentially as the network expands. Well, we're putting that principle to work in the performance process this year. We're

> *crowdsourcing the performance review. That means everyone is going to have a say, and a stake, in the performance process."*
>
> *"Ask yourself this question," Rebecca said. "What if everyone you came in contact with, all through your work day, in any division or team at Hydrolab, had a say in your performance review with ongoing positive feedback? What would that mean for you and your team?"*

As I introduced earlier, the last decade has seen the rise of a fascinating trend: the marriage of data from multiple sources and individual opinions to create the entirely new form of decision making called *crowdsourcing*. It's everywhere, from "star rankings" on Amazon.com's product pages to services like Angie's List, Zagat.com, and TripAdvisor. Now people make decisions based on feedback from dozens, hundreds, or tens of thousands of other people. And these crowdsourced conclusions are supplementing "expert" opinions because they are more accurate.

In the same decade, the spread of social media has opened new channels and habits of communication. Facebook, Yammer, Yelp, LinkedIn, and other services make crowd communication—many people sharing information with many others in innumerable ways—the new language of business.

In his bestselling 2004 book, *The Wisdom of Crowds*, business journalist James Surowiecki made a compelling case for an astonishing idea: "*Under the right circumstances*, groups are remarkably intelligent, and are often smarter than the smartest people in them."[1] [Italics mine.] In case after case, Surowiecki showed that aggregating and analyzing the diverse impressions, opinions, beliefs, and even predictions of a large group of people acting individually gave more accurate solutions to a problem than relying on a single expert.

To illustrate his thesis, Surowiecki cited the observation of nineteenth-century English polymath Francis Galton, who witnessed people at a country fair trying to guess the weight of an ox. When all predictions were collected, the mathematical average turned out to be closer to the actual weight than any individual guess.

In a more recent, deliberately simple experiment, 56 students were asked to estimate the number of beans in a jar. The average of their prediction—871—was closer to the actual number of 850 than any individual estimate.

"Under the right circumstances" is a key phrase in Surowiecki's description above. Harnessing the wisdom of crowds is different from polling; it requires the active interest and participation of an appropriate large group, and the data have to be safeguarded against misinterpretation.

We've seen a lot of businesses use Surowiecki's analysis to unlock value in collective wisdom, from crowdsourcing product improvements to capitalizing new ventures.[2] Facebook, Twitter, and the like have created entire virtual worlds whose purpose is to leverage the "wisdom" of large audiences for entertainment, insight, and information. Virtual "stock markets" such as the Iowa Electronic Markets use crowdsourcing to predict elections and monetary policy.[3]

All Kinds of Crowds

Less than a decade after Surowiecki brought the wisdom of crowds to public attention, businesses applied the idea in such endeavors as:

- *Crowdfunding*, in which individuals propose a business or not-for-profit endeavor online and seek investors or donors. The crowd decides which are the best investments/causes by choosing which to support. Examples: Kickstarter.com and DonorsChoose.org.
- *Crowdsolving*, in which a problem is posed and many work on solutions. In 2012, GE provided complex data sets to the public in an open competition to predict airliners' arrival on the runway and at the gate. Examples: Phylo, Kaggle.com.
- *Crowdbuilding*, in which a complex problem or process is broken into component parts, and many people compete or cooperate to build each part. This operates like standard subcontracting with

the difference being the naming of a winner after the work is done. Example: the creation of Linux.

■ *Crowdcreating*, in which creative work such as logo or clothing design is performed in a marketplace, with either individual clients or the crowd deciding the commercial value of creative solutions. Examples: 99designs.com, threadless.com.

Crowds are not spontaneously smart or accurate, as anyone who has been stuck in traffic knows. Four conditions optimize the wisdom of crowds in practice, and not incidentally they are also hallmarks of a robust organizational culture:

■ *Diversity of thought, opinion, and information,* so that many points of view and observations feed decision making
■ *Independence of thought and opinion,* with participants contributing based on their best judgment and not "groupthink"
■ *Decentralization of information,* so that the richest possible set of information can be collected
■ *Aggregation of individual thoughts and opinions* in a meaningful context, to interpret them accurately

Internet-based technology makes crowd applications possible because it connects people in a flexible network of interactions and enables interpretation of the data gathered. Much more data are generated from multiple sources, rendering a richer picture of reality.

Looking at corporate applications of the wisdom of crowds, Surowiecki pointed out the crucial differences between what companies tend to do versus what markets tend to do:

Companies tend to pay people based on what they're expected to do. In a market, people get paid based simply on what they do. . . . Top-down corporations give people an incentive to hide information and dissemble. . . . Markets encourage people to find new valuable information and then let everyone else know about it. And this, too, is what corporations should be looking for: ways to provide their employees with the incentive to uncover and act on private information.[4]

Those last two words are loaded with meaning. Surowiecki defines private information as more than concrete facts: "It can also include interpretation, analysis, or even intuition."[5] This is a perfect description of the broad scope of "eyewitness" evidence when gauging performance. When everyone is encouraged to shine a light on everyone else's positive business behaviors, everyone adds their interpretation, analysis, and even intuition to a growing profile of each person's performance. This social recognition uncovers and spotlights great performance that might otherwise be seen by a small, select few—the eyewitnesses who happen to be nearby or directly affected.

This is the value of social recognition in managing performance: Unlike a corporate hierarchy, social recognition creates a *market-based* system of assessing employees. Crowdsourcing input about employee performance creates a market composed of every employee reacting to other employees. Social recognition is the transaction engine of that market, and the currency is information about performance.

> *Crowdsourcing input about employee performance creates a market composed of every employee, and social recognition is the transaction engine of that market.*

To apply Surowiecki's thesis to performance management, it's necessary to more narrowly define three concepts and their relationships:

1. *Social recognition* in performance management means both gathering data about positive behavior (crowdsourcing) and interpreting those data (using the wisdom of crowds) to create meaningful conclusions about performance.

2. *Crowdsourcing* means assembling a large amount of data made up of many individual inputs (such as selecting 56 students to individually estimate the number of beans in a jar).

3. *The wisdom of crowds* means processing and interpreting those data in a meaningful way (collecting the bean estimates and averaging them).

Applying the three concepts sequentially to create meaningful input to a performance review looks like what is shown in Figure 2.1.

A workplace group practicing social recognition creates crowdsourced data with many specific recognition moments—those times when an employee formally recognizes someone else's effort or accomplishment. Many moments together aggregate in the system to create a crowdsourced—and crowd-wise—average for each individual's performance along a spectrum of qualities. These averages can function both as input to individual performance and a higher-level group average. (We walk through the process in more detail in Chapter 7).

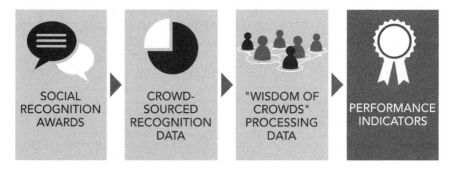

Figure 2.1 Many recognition awards taken together creates performance indicators.

Networks Give More Information

Crowdsourcing a performance review means getting social input about someone's work behaviors from different sources. There are four basic communication models among people, based on how many people are giving input and how many are receiving that input, and you can graph them as shown in Figure 2.2.

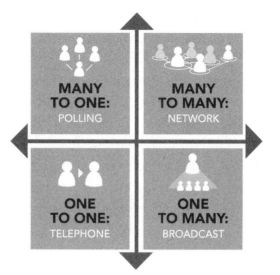

Figure 2.2 The four basic communication models

The upper-right quadrant represents a network with many participants, and the lower-left a one-to-one conversation. Obviously the network contains much more information. Translate this model to performance management, and the chart looks like Figure 2.3.

Figure 2.3 Four basic performance review models

At the lower left of the figure is the traditional manager-to-employee performance review. The conversation is based only on information from those two people. At the upper right is a rich environment in which all individuals can contribute performance information. (For the sake of illustration, the upper left cites the "360-degree review" which is essentially a panel reviewing an individual, and the lower right represents a manager reviewing team performance.)

This is not an action plan—yet. The figure illustrates the much greater amount of data available to a manager in the network model. The information must be relevant (that's the job of social recognition) and understood (that's the job of social recognition software, the manager, and company culture).

Many Subjective Opinions—A Picture of Performance

By harnessing the wisdom of crowds, many subjective observations taken together provide a more objective (and accurate) picture of an employee's performance than a single subjective judgment. Managers are notified throughout the year of employees' good work even if they don't witness it firsthand. And their possible subjectivity is tempered by what the crowd says about the work.

A social recognition program funnels many subjective impressions into an objective performance review because the recognition moments are conceptually tied to individual and company values and goals. It averages out prejudice or baggage on the part of both manager and employee. The data act as a check-and-balance mechanism for each individual manager's strengths and shortcomings in gauging performance.

A social recognition program funnels many subjective impressions into an objective performance review.

Done right, a crowdsourced performance system also reveals gaps in skills or performance. For example, an employee might believe he has great team skills because he's widely liked, but the crowd could remain silent on this, instead recognizing only individual acts or skills. Noticing that nobody sees the employee as a team player, the manager can address the issue with objectivity. This doesn't mean that the employee is subverting teamwork; it might simply be a lack of emphasis on getting things done with others, which is a common problem with less experienced team leaders. The ensuing dialogue is enriched by anecdote and positive feedback.

Social recognition raises group consciousness about the right behaviors. Rather than withholding information about what to do and when to do it, social recognition distributes that information to all participants. This conforms well to the modern, decentralized organization and overcomes a potential problem.

According to Surowiecki, the problem with most decentralized organizations is that valuable information found in one group is not necessarily shared across the system. Social recognition's shared data achieve an ideal state that Surowiecki describes as "a way for individuals . . . to aggregate that local knowledge and private information into a collective whole, much as Google relies on the local knowledge of millions of webpage operators to make Google searches ever smarter and ever quicker."[6]

A Culture of Collaboration: What Does Crowdsourcing Mean for Human Resources?

Today, we're on the leading edge of a major change in how companies are managed. Strategic leaders are talking about social hierarchies and social, community-based styles of collaboration and goal setting. Companies are engaging their own internal information markets (the private information of their employees) in grassroots versions of management, as opposed to purely executive-driven, inflexible, hierarchical management.

Great managers know that knowledge is more valuable than facts alone. At work, knowledge is not simply memorizing facts but also manipulating facts, experience, intuition, understanding, insight, memories, impressions, and feelings. Knowledge is shared by social contact and is manifested in behaviors, not words.

In practice, social recognition means that peers are inspired to publicly recognize each other's accomplishments on an ongoing basis. Good performance, large and small, inspires peers to publicly approve and broadcast the behavior while recognizing the person responsible. Performance is explicitly linked to job goals and company values, and that link is based on all the components of knowledge (experience, intuition, insight, etc.), not rigid, preconceived scenarios.

Each recognition insight benefits the employee and his or her manager. Over time, the collective insights of the crowd create incredible value for the organization.

"The wisdom of crowds can tell you a lot," explains Joanna Geraghty, executive vice president and chief people officer of JetBlue. "It can tell you whether somebody is an influencer. It can tell you whether somebody truly delivers a lot of extraordinary moments. Looking at that data and developing programs around that—whether it is thank-you programs or compensation programs—I think there are limitless things you can do when you start looking at what the wisdom of the crowds can tell you."[7]

With a mechanism to harness the wisdom of crowds, a large amount of new data about individual behaviors, on a number of dimensions, would be available for performance reviews. More significantly for HR, those data can be collated and analyzed for multiple purposes, for example, creating work teams including skills and experience, and also temperamental factors like willingness to share information or a tendency toward initiative. Today's HR executive looks to assessment testing and the observations of managers (as well as work results) to gain this information. Adding a wisdom-of-crowds system that creates a mosaic of every employee gives HR and the managers it advises more data.

It's significant to HR that all these data about individuals are based on observed behaviors and on facts, not opinions. This is reminiscent of behavior-based interviewing, familiar to every HR manager, which suggests that past work behaviors are the best predictors of future behaviors. Behavior-based interviewing has earned the respect of a generation of

HR executives, and crowdsourced performance assessment is built on exactly the same logic.

The bigger changes brought on by crowdsourcing performance management are cultural. True collaboration is characterized by trust, positivity, and shared responsibility. This is the cultural opposite of a traditional, top-down performance review regimen. It is also a good aspirational definition of a twenty-first-century workplace, not because everybody has to feel good but because trust, positivity, and shared responsibility are foundations of fast-moving, creative, and energetic business cultures.

The pace of change alone is argument enough that a culture of collaboration is needed in order for an organization to compete.

The crowdsourced performance review reimagines the performance review system by adding cultural practices and habits that keep pace with the changes in business thinking and technology. Performance management using the wisdom of crowds requires a cultural bias toward collaboration. For millennial employees, this is a natural extension of the social media and social work habits discussed in Chapter 1. Others will have to change their habits.

In practice, everyone involved has to offer his or her positive opinion about performance. Social recognition aggregates the opinions and thoughts of many individuals to arrive at a richer, more accurate conclusion than one person alone could attain. The key is to reach a critical mass of employees participating by offering "star rankings" (like those rankings mentioned in Chapter 1) of others' performance in a managed system. Participation should be at least 80 percent for the system to reach maximum effectiveness.

Workers who fear personal risk in offering their opinions of others might be less inclined to participate; this is one reason why a social recognition system is based on positive reaction. But reassuring the timid is not enough for most workplaces, and people who are not used to sharing openly need to acquire the habit of observing and noting good performance in others.

A culture of collaboration also means that no single person comes up with the ultimate, definitive assessment of someone's performance.

This is anathema to old-fashioned executives and micromanagers. Their resistance is based on a misperception that using the wisdom of crowds robs them of authority and accountability.

That's not the case. Managers are fundamentally charged with achieving work goals through others. They need to realize that the additional information created by a social recognition system empowers them to make wiser decisions about performance, decisions that range beyond the old pigeonholes of A, B, C ratings and offer a nuanced and actionable narrative of each employee's behavior.

Executive Insight

"Culture is a slow-growing tree. In the beginning it needs protection. But after a couple of decades the culture will be stronger than you are. You need to work with it, not against it.

"Culture is a powerful but fragile thing. If you burn down the culture tree, it takes a long time to grow another one."
—Wally Bock, Three Star Leadership[8]

Collaboration is a business process movement much larger than HR or performance management. As we've seen, it is a set of enabling technologies and habits that extend a manager's ability to make the right decisions.

You can think of social recognition as a healthy-living routine for company culture. It promotes only desired behaviors and discourages superfluous or unhealthy behaviors. It finds positive cultural clues in work behaviors large and small. Properly implemented, it also differentiates among efforts, distributing rewards for behaviors proportionate to their impact.

At its core, social recognition democratizes performance management. In a company, 90 percent of activities have eyewitnesses who see successful work because it affects them, but too often the manager hasn't seen it and the eyewitnesses don't have management responsibility or accountability to reward or recognize that behavior. To *democratize* performance recognition is to give everyone an incentive to improve performance across the board—to give everyone access to "catch someone doing something good."

We will turn to the matter of culture in Chapter 4, but first we must ask, what might motivate people to collaborate in business? What might allow people to perform at higher levels? In an information economy, what is the juice that unleashes higher levels of creativity and innovation? Financial reward? Prestige? Ego? The answer is even more basic than that.

The answer is happiness.

3

The Currency of Happiness

Trevor set out in 1999 to build not only a successful business but also a great company. He studied examples from business best-sellers and conducted a private correspondence with two professors of organizational psychology from his MBA days. He worked hard to put five principles in place even in the early years, when Hydrolab profits were meager but employee morale was high. They were:

- *Safe employees and safe customers*
- *Show focus and determination.*
- *Demonstrate integrity daily.*
- *Nurture engagement, energy and enthusiasm.*
- *Unite in execution.*

Trevor was proud of Hydrolab's success, but as the company reached its tenth anniversary, Trevor could see how much harder it was to maintain that fourth principle. Finding energy and inspiration was easier in a start-up with 50 people than a global company of 8,500 employees. Even higher profits, benefits, and pay weren't enough to bring back that early sense of energy and engagement. And as new Hydrolab offices opened and staff numbers grew, he knew he couldn't be the only cheerleader for a great and lasting culture. There were too many employees to reach one to one.

In 2009, Trevor hired Rebecca as a C-level HR partner, reporting directly to him, and he gave her the specific charter to maintain a Positivity Dominated Workplace. She'd done a lot— with global cultural initiatives, a first-rate recognition program, tailored benefits, and other great work, but the performance management process had remained stubbornly resistant to change until now.

At the 2012 executive retreat, Trevor asked Rebecca to propose an overhaul of the performance review system. She had come up with an intriguing idea: Instead of scrapping the system entirely, she would connect performance management with the growing recognition platform around the world.

"I get the connection between recognition and culture," said Trevor, "But what's the connection between recognition and performance?" Trevor asked.

Rebecca replied, "Energy. Spirit. And ultimately happiness. When every one of 8,500 employees is on the lookout for the behaviors that make us successful, you'll get a rising tide of good feeling and a rising awareness of what great performance means.

"When people are recognized for doing the right thing, they feel happy. And then they want to do more of the right thing, which means better performance."

Rebecca concluded with a wry smile. "As someone I know named Trevor would say, 'Another blinding flash of the obvious.'"

In April 2012 more than 600 government officials, academics, civil and religious leaders gathered at United Nations headquarters to hear a diminutive man from one of the world's poorest countries discuss a new paradigm for national development. The man was Prime Minister Jigmi Y. Thinley of Bhutan, a tiny Himalayan kingdom, and he was there to discuss happiness.

Since 2005, Bhutan has experimented with an alternative to gross domestic product (GDP) as a national metric of progress. Its index measures gross national happiness (GNH), which expands the GDP model of economic activity to include additional domains such as ecological vitality, educational attainment, health, quality of governance, emotional/psychological wel-lbeing, and time use. The careful model of GNH at www.grossnationalhappiness.com dispels the notion that this is a gauzy dream of a Buddhist/Hindu Shangri-La; the discipline of Bhutan's proposition has won serious study. Happiness might be both measurable and a better metric of how a country is doing than statistics limited to transactions in the marketplace. To mangle an Enlightenment phrase, perhaps people have a right to something more profound than "life, liberty, and the pursuit of gross domestic product."

I'd like to change your mind about happiness at work. It is not the result of profit (profit is the fuel of business, not its purpose). It is not the result of pay (pay is the employer's half of a transaction, and performance is the employee's half). It is not even the result of financial success (success gives satisfaction, but the world has plenty of unhappy millionaires).

Happiness is the *facilitator* of success. If that sounds like a bit too New-Agey for a business concept, I hasten to point out that dozens of studies demonstrate that happy people at work drive success, and profit, and durable competitive advantage. I believe that a company's best operating advantage is to create happiness at work. From that, every performance goal can flow. Failing that, every effort to promote greater performance falters.

It is a huge structural theme in business today. It's a legitimate area for scientific pursuit and research. Business leaders realize that happiness at work is worth exploring because it boosts financial performance, employee retention, and corporate durability.

> ### Executive Insight
>
> People with higher well-being are more agile. And part of agility is resilience, or the ability to bounce back after a problem." Agility is valuable when workers are forced to adapt to tough times. In uncertain times, agility helps people solve problems and innovate—fundamental requirements for companies trying to grow.[1]
>
> —Jim Harter, Gallup's Chief Scientist of
> Employee Engagement and Well-Being

Consider Tony Hsieh, CEO of Zappos and author of *Delivering Happiness*.[2] Nobody would care about how quirky the Zappos "happiness culture" was if it had gone out of business six months after it started. But Hsieh built a powerful company in a merciless industry (online retail), and Amazon bought Zappos for almost a billion dollars. People are paying attention.

What Makes Happiness?

You might be thinking of happiness as a state of carefree pleasure or satisfaction, or of ease, but these elements are not necessary to happiness.

Tal Ben-Shahar is a researcher and lecturer whose research specialty is happiness, and his courses on positive psychology and the psychology of leadership were among the most popular ever taught at Harvard. His studies suggest that happiness is achieved by a sustainable set of conditions.[3] Three of his six keys to happiness are especially relevant to performance management:

- *Happiness lies at the intersection of pleasure and meaning.* Happy and engaged people enjoy what they are doing and believe it to be personally significant.

■ *Happiness depends on a person's state of mind.* Day to day, people choose to ascribe positive or negative attributes to events, and their sense of well-being depends largely on these perceptions. For example, when a manager offers a compliment for work well done, it's typical for the employee to feel gratification. When a manager offers constructive criticism, does the employee see that as failure or as an opportunity to grow and progress? In both cases, the interpretation can determine happiness more than the bare facts can.

■ *Expressing gratitude promotes personal happiness.* Business consultants, etiquette experts, and religious leaders have long known that saying "thank you" promotes everyone's happiness. Now psychological studies confirm the two-way benefits of expressed gratitude. Giving recognition and thanks for a job well done promotes happiness in both the recipient and the giver.

> *Giving recognition and thanks for a job well done promotes happiness in both the recipient and the giver.*

In the book *Stumbling on Happiness,*[4] Harvard psychologist Dan Gilbert points out that making visible progress toward a goal promotes happiness as well. Now think about those intense work times when the team is all pulling together and its total focus on creating something amazing keeps team members working after midnight. A lot of those happiness boxes are ticked off in those heroic times: Feeling like you're progressing toward a goal, feeling optimistic; feeling like you're part of something bigger than the day-to-day work; and feeling like you're being supported and supporting others.

Those are legendary times at a company, and notice that people are sustained through them, hour by hour, by the conviction and affirmation that they are making progress toward the goal. Happiness comes both from the end goal and making progress.

Harvard Business School professor Teresa Amabile and researcher Steven Kramer, coauthors of *The Progress Principle*, asked 238 professionals in seven different countries to keep diaries recording their psychological state through the workday. In a summary of their findings for *The New York Times*, they wrote, "Conventional wisdom suggests that pressure enhances performance; our real-time data, however, shows that workers perform better when they are happily engaged in what they do. . . . A clear pattern emerged when we analyzed the 64,000 specific workday events reported in the diaries: of all the events that engage people at work, the single most important—by far—is simply making progress in meaningful work."[5]

This research suggests the importance of frequent, timely recognition of progress. Managers, peers, and others who reinforce the significance and meaning of even incremental progress to one another build momentum in goodwill and good feeling. Contrast that practice with exhortations or ratings in a once-a-year performance review. Which practice promotes happiness and therefore productivity?

Lest readers think I'm glossing over the struggles of work, I'll comment that researchers also distinguish between momentary happiness and the long-term belief that one is happy. To put this in a business context, consider that those heroic all-nighters have a lot of stressful moments and hours of disappointment or frustration as well as triumph. Not every moment is pleasurable, but the people who are supporting each other through the process report that their outlook is happy (and confident, and self-congratulatory, and all the rest). They are positive.

Promoting happiness is not a matter of having it easy. On the contrary, much happiness for entrepreneurs and others takes place in highly uncertain environments, when progress is all you have to promote belief.

Confirmed by rigorous study and common experience, happiness in the workplace is an advantage, and managers know it. They intuitively know they will get higher morale leading to higher productivity, higher performance, and ultimately better financial performance. It boils down to a logic tree like the one shown in Figure 3.1.

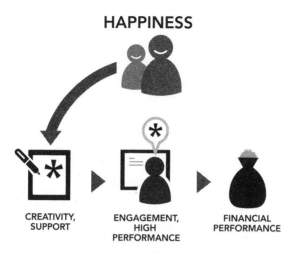

HAPPINESS

CREATIVITY, SUPPORT ▶ ENGAGEMENT, HIGH PERFORMANCE ▶ FINANCIAL PERFORMANCE

Figure 3.1 The path to financial performance begins with workplace happiness.

How to promote happiness becomes the next question. Is it a matter of paying people more? Or finding motivated employees in the first place? Or is it a matter of removing obstacles to achievement? Does it require initiative and engagement? All these promote happiness, and these and more actions are essentially components of a larger cultural phenomenon I call a *Positivity Dominated Workplace.* In a Positivity Dominated Workplace, everyone is invested in promoting a culture of possibility, opportunity, achievement, security, risk-taking, or any other combination of traits that define a company culture.

Positivity encourages happiness over time. The field of positive psychology affirms this across many fields, from business to physical health. In the next section, we see how happiness and positivity can manifest themselves in a business through the practice of social recognition.

Life, Liberty, and the Pursuit of . . . a Paycheck?

The well-known hierarchy of human needs observed by psychologist Abraham Maslow provides a template for thinking about recognition's effectiveness and place in management's tool kit. Here is a simplified version of that model:

A Hierarchy of Human Needs

Maslow's famous hierarchy (see Figure 3.2) begins with those needs related to physical survival (the most basic needs) and climbs through the needs for safety, social contact, self-esteem, recognition, and status. The highest need (and psychological achievement) is called self-actualization.

Figure 3.2 Maslow's hierarchy of human needs

Proponents of recognition in business point out that recognition satisfies the higher needs Maslow described. In fact, Maslow's pyramid can be seen as a metaphor for what a workplace can potentially provide, from the pay that ensures food and shelter, to safety and social contact, to self-esteem. Self-actualization in the organization can be seen in those who love their work, who find their identity and satisfaction from their work, and who are "a perfect fit" with the organization.

The higher you climb in Maslow's hierarchy, the more individualized the needs become. Physical needs are pretty much the same no matter who the person is—everyone needs food and water. Safety needs are more individual, but there are plenty of guidelines for creating a physically and psychologically safe workplace. Social needs require a workplace that functions socially, in which company culture encourages socially productive interactions (peer-to-peer recognition *is* a socially productive interaction). Esteem needs and self-actualization are unique to everyone.

Recognition feeds the higher social and psychic needs of individuals, to drive them to performance above and beyond just what's listed in their job description. When an individual feels that his or her work is valued by a manager, that specific behaviors are rewarded, that the workplace is fulfilling, engagement follows.

Executive Insight

"What [Tony Hsieh] really cares about is making Zappos.com's employees and customers feel really, really good because he has decided that his entire business revolves around one thing: happiness. Everything at Zappos.com serves that end.

"Zappos.com's 1,300 employees talk about the place with a religious fervor. The phrase *core values* can prompt emotional soliloquies, and the CEO is held with a regard typically afforded rock stars and cult leaders."[6]

—*Inc.* Magazine, May 1, 2009

A Hierarchy of Employee Needs

Intuit created an insightful hierarchy of employee needs as part of its leadership model. Referring to the relationship between Intuit and its employees, the hierarchy begins with basic needs for security and justice and then climbs to the needs for accomplishment, connection, and inspiration (see Figure 3.3).

There is much management wisdom to be gained from this chart. For our purpose, let's note that Intuit believes that recognition of the right behaviors is a tool for promoting, encouraging, and confirming *all* these needs.

Figure 3.3 Intuit's hierarchy of needs

It's no wonder that Intuit—where in a special survey conducted by the Total Rewards department, 93 percent of employees agree that the company's recognition program helps motivate sustained high performance—has been a "Best Place to Work" on the annual *Fortune* magazine list for years.

The mediocre manager likes to think that his or her employees should be grateful to have a job. Perhaps they are, but that attitude has culture management backwards. In a well-run company, the organization and the individual manager acting on its behalf harness the power of appreciation not by receiving it, but by giving it to the employees.

Let's look at the aspects of appreciation that make it essential to culture management:

- *Appreciation is motivating.* People like being thanked. It feels good to affirm employees' worth and value. How do they get more thanks? By repeating the behavior that wins the thanks.

- *Appreciation is humanizing.* The ability to express appreciation is a key strength in a leader. Appreciation is an emotion that, in many cultures, actually lends power to someone else, in the expectation that he or she will receive it. Can you imagine having your thanks rejected? It makes the person saying "thank you" a little less exalted, a little more human.
- *Appreciation is specific.* "Thank you" is reacting to a specific act, achievement, or attitude that's recognized in the transaction. It also lends credence to the importance and value of that act.
- *Appreciation is empowering.* First, appreciation empowers by affirming the power of the individual to make a choice. (I don't have to earn your appreciation, but I choose to.) Second, because appreciation can be expressed by anyone in the hierarchy to anyone else in the hierarchy, it is a reward that potentially cuts across the class and culture lines of an organization.
- *Appreciation is powerful.* Spiritual leaders emphasize the importance of gratitude on the path to wholeness. National leaders thank soldiers for their service; mayors offer the thanks of a grateful public to first responders to emergency situations. And notice how often the most enlightened business leaders attribute their success openly and often to their employees. Appreciation establishes a psychological contract between employees. Complete that contract, and you are assured of more productive relations among workers. Break that contract, and you are assured of higher turnover, lower engagement, and a population of employees who delivers below its full potential.

Recognition as an Indicator of Company Health

It's ironic that many executives who accept the power of branding, which is an appeal to customer emotions, ignore the power of employee emotion. Perhaps the intangible benefits of work—like a sense of belonging or a sense that one's job brings meaning beyond a paycheck—seem too easily dismissed as "just touchy-feely stuff." Human capital management, however, means applying management methodology to the emotional needs and power of humans.

Recognition is particularly adaptable to the goals of management. Recognition done right improves retention of key employees, improves performance of all employees by guiding behavior, motivates the already-engaged employee to deeper engagement, and inspires both the recipient and others who witness the accolade.

The End of Loyalty?

Are you only *retaining* employees or are you creating *loyal* employees? What's the difference?

"A survey by the Center for Work-Life Policy, a U.S. consultancy, found that between June 2007 and December 2008 the proportion of employees who professed loyalty to their employers slumped from 95 percent to 39 percent; the number voicing trust in them fell from 79 percent to 22 percent. A more recent survey by DDI, another U.S. consultancy, found that more than half of respondents described their job as 'stagnant,' meaning that they had nothing interesting to do and little hope of promotion. Half of these 'stagnators' planned to look for another job as soon as the economy improved. People are both clinging to their current jobs, however much they dislike them, and dreaming of moving when the economy improves. This is taking a toll on both short-term productivity and long-term competitiveness: The people most likely to move when things look up are high-flyers who feel that their talents are being ignored."[7]

Employees agree to be retained in a tough economic environment or in other situations in which options may be limited. But if you're not fostering employee loyalty, as soon as more options become available, you will see your employee retention numbers plummet.

Employees Expect More Than a Paycheck

Have you ever worked in an organization in which management talks about what the culture is, and the employees silently think, "Yeah, yeah, you speak about company values, but your behavior says otherwise." This cynicism in the face of management is epidemic. It's one reason we laugh at Dilbert cartoons. It's one reason for public outrage at how irresponsible financial practices worldwide caused the Great Recession of 2008–2009. On the other hand, executives who show authenticity by facing the brutal truth in a forthright manner or who give every employee, no matter his or her position, a stake in the company's growth (as when Google's on-site massage therapist became a millionaire through the company's stock options) engender legitimacy. These acts of authenticity, of living values with integrity, even to the point of sacrificing some reward, give enormous power to their authority. Employees in survey after survey say that they want to work for an authentic, open, and appreciative culture.

The Positivity Dominated Workplace

I ask human resources people to imagine a Positivity Dominated Workplace, and they immediately think it's a high-performing workplace. They don't have to reason through the psychologists' studies; they just immediately make the connection. HR executives understand that positivity creates the right culture for happiness to take root and flourish. This feeds energy, productivity, creativity, and high performance, which is ultimately linked with financial performance. Social recognition, as we've discussed, promotes a culture of positivity because its nature is positive. To expand the logic tree we saw earlier, social recognition leads ultimately to better financial performance. (See Figure 3.4.)

I have seen this time and again as social recognition programs are instituted in companies. A happy, more positive culture replicates itself, feeds on itself, and is self-reinforcing thus creating a flywheel effect or virtuous cycle. There's an insatiable appetite in companies for goodwill, for positive interaction. The more you feed that or the more you allow

Figure 3.4 Social recognition leads to better financial performance.

it to flourish, the more it takes the attention in a company. You'll never eliminate negativity altogether—it's just part of some temperaments—but it becomes less and less influential as the benefits of a Positivity Dominated Workplace become evident.

The key to putting a Positivity Dominated Workplace into action is the "social" part of social recognition. Giving thanks is a key to happiness—the cornerstone, the social part, of social recognition. In the next chapter, we see how performance can be recognized and improved every day by crowdsourcing a culture of positivity in the workplace.

4

Crowdsourcing Performance with Social Recognition

Nobody had ever accused Liz of being a gut-feel manager. Liz liked data and liked to tell the software engineers and project managers who reported to her that facts were the foundation of good management. "If you can measure it, you can manage it" was her motto. But nobody had ever accused Liz of being a cold-hearted automaton, either, and now she felt personal concern for her team.

Everybody's goals and priorities for 2014 were about to change. Hydrolab had announced the acquisition of its largest competitor, GeoClean, a friendly merger but an incredibly complex one.

"Well, that's life in the big bad world of business," she thought. In January your work was all about clobbering the competition, and in February you found out your work was all about welcoming the competition and integrating its products to yours.

What to manage? What to measure? Liz sketched a change management grid on a graph pad. She would need to phase in program and quality management on a new integration team, create new goals for job descriptions, and get everything ready to go in the next few months. Designing the process for measurement was easy enough; what about the people and their goals?

At her computer, Liz scanned the social recognition graph of her team, looking for key qualities that would help in the integration. She could see the unexpected influence of a younger member of the project management team, Dana. Liz thought Dana was talented but hadn't had time to think about her leadership capabilities, but Dana's peers kept mentioning her focus and take-charge attitude. Dana might be up for a challenge, thought Liz.

Robert was an obvious choice for a program management role. Liz liked the precision of his work, and integration with Geo-Clean would mean tracking 10,000 details. She had already recognized him publicly for that.

To her surprise, a guy in engineering named Tony kept coming up in the database for a possible role she hadn't even considered. She thought, "Let's keep track of Tony's 'quest for elegant code' that's noted here in the system."

Liz searched her team's social recognition scores and comments for an hour, studying the surprising patterns that emerged when the work of 28 people was recorded. She realized with pride that she was reading a story, a narrative of a department that worked pretty damn well. They'd be ready to take on the integration later in the year.

Gordon Bell is a computer scientist. Maybe that's all you care to know about him, but if you want to know more, he can tell you. For 14 years Bell has recorded his every telephone call and conversation. A digital camera swinging from his neck snaps a picture every 60 seconds. He has retained hundreds of thousands of documents, web pages—everything that has passed before his eyes or ears since 1998. Bell has even recorded his movements with a GPS device in those years. Wonder where Gordon Bell was and what he was doing on your last birthday? He can tell you.

Bell, a 78-year-old former executive currently with Microsoft, is the patron saint of a curious cadre of "lifeloggers," who preserve every detail of their lives (members of a subcadre broadcast their every move and conversation on the web and are called, inevitably, "lifebloggers"). Unlike chronic hoarders, who acquire and hold onto objects neurotically, life-loggers are conducting a long experiment with the mind in general and memory in particular. Bell's thesis: What if you didn't have to remember anything? It's the big data concept focused on a single life.

Lifeloggers wear cameras, carry smartphones and tablets and other sensors (some record physical data—weight, pulse, etc.), all hooked up to infinite storage. Everything that takes place in their lives is recorded in huge databases. Bell believes that this information, when searched and analyzed, is a key to a completely different human experience.[1] Imagine, for example, if you could collect in one place pictures or notes about every time you felt happy in the last ten years. What if you could look at those moments as a narrative, unclouded by the vagaries of memory or habit? What would you do with that information?

The lifelogging experiment includes the big data elite. Google's Project Glass will release a wearable minicamera in 2013 resembling minimalist eyeglasses that also include a tiny display. The wearer can get information about a location or an object via voice command. It will begin as a novelty item (with a high price tag) but the commercialization of this notion—and Google's unmatched ability to do creative things with data—will lead people to contemplate what could be done when perfect recall is just a mouse click (or a voice command) away. (At the 2013 South by Southwest (SXSW) conference, Swedish startup Memoto got a lot of buzz with its tiny automatic lifelogging camera.[2])

How might a business use a concept like lifelogging?

Imagine that your business could record all the moments of real innovation, and starting from the moment that innovation appeared, move out in concentric circles to examine what led to that innovation. Even a simple action like saving money on a purchase has a long thread of events, conversations, e-mails, calculations, and interactions among employees. If you knew what those conditions were, could you replicate them to inspire further innovations?

Consider how intelligent retrieval of every moment might change a business. Executives could ask, "Who were the key people in our iPhone/ Android app project? That project was hugely successful; how did the people interact? What did we do that we should replicate? And how did that project compare with the less successful initiatives?" Even two years after the fact, data analytics could delve into the collective "memory bank" and call up everyone who was involved.

Compare that to the traditional performance review where almost no behavior has been recorded. Outcomes are on the record but not the behaviors that led to those outcomes, and certainly not the mindset or company culture that facilitated those outcomes. Managers can't remember all the behaviors because they weren't there to witness them.

At best, the traditional performance review asks an employee, six or ten months after the fact, "How did you do that?" There's no context; there's little detail. Even worse, human memory is prone to changing the facts to fit a desired narrative (as any trial lawyer will tell you). When a manager and an employee rely on memory to reconstruct how a great project worked out, they begin with limited data. A crowdsourced social recognition practice can relate all the obvious and hidden behaviors that led to that great outcome.

A manager might point out that there are many ways to achieve a goal. That observation might be true, but it does nothing to improve performance. There are even more ways to fail. Knowing how a goal was attained is the central understanding of "best practices" training and the core of improving performance.

A robust performance review should include a regression analysis, the discipline of understanding how past events led to the present situation. A manager should be able to point to a success and ask, "What made this project succeed so well? What did you do differently that time?

What did you learn, and how did you apply it to the next project?" The review process should be able to suggest answers to each of those questions objectively, because the heart of regression analysis is factual data. And those data come from many observations by many witnesses recording the events in real time.

Those data are generated by social recognition, and it's not just a data-gathering mechanism but a cultural solution to the limitations of the performance review.

The holy grail of performance management is a culture that creates and sustains high achievement. Social recognition serves as a healthy-living routine for company culture. It promotes only desired behaviors and discourages superfluous or unhealthy behaviors. Properly implemented, it also differentiates among efforts, distributing rewards for behaviors proportional to their impact.

> *The holy grail of performance management is a culture that creates and sustains high achievement.*

A high-performance culture promotes great performance by inspiring feelings of satisfaction. This is described by Dov Seidman in his bestselling book, *How: Why HOW We Do Anything Means Everything*,[3] in which he demonstrates that employees achieve a mission and feel significant when they are aligned with the culture. Culture empowers self-management. Culture encourages positive behaviors even more than management by objective (MBO) or incentive plans.

When people record positive behaviors, they are also lifelogging the most positive activities of the company from many different points of view. Everyone is reinforcing for themselves and others the significance of the company's values and how behavior is aligned with those values.

Social recognition democratizes performance management. In a company, most activities have eyewitnesses who see successful work because it affects them, but too often the manager hasn't seen it and the eyewitnesses don't have management responsibility or accountability to reward or recognize that behavior. To democratize performance recognition is to give everyone a stake in performance improvement.

Coping with Change

The traditional performance review is structured to list goals and behaviors at the beginning of the year and to judge performance by how it hits those goals. This works for rating some factors, but what about goals and behaviors that cannot be predicted? Business changes at the speed of light these days, and if employees are working to the job description, changing with the times is much more difficult. Without adaptability, the organization risks "doing the wrong thing more efficiently every year." By locking down the criteria by which an employee will be judged, the traditional review brings a formal inflexibility to business, leaving managers with the dilemma of either adapting the system on the fly or disregarding it altogether.

Here's an example that occurs over a calendar year: All the job descriptions with goals and targets are set in January, and the company from top to bottom is focused on revenue growth. Months later, a sudden downturn in the economy forces the company to pivot from growth to cost containment. (Many companies experienced precisely this scenario in September 2008.) All employees are tasked with reducing costs. Suddenly all the goals set by HR and the managers are out of step with reality. At the end of the year, it might be possible to add cost containment to each job description, but how can managers quantify an employee's efforts in this? How should managers rate an employee on January's revenue goals that could not be met because of cost-cutting? Without a midyear change in every job description, market conditions will undermine the relevance of the traditional review. And as the company pivots, there's no time to change every job description.

In this situation, social recognition broadens the scope of the traditional review to *immediately recognize, reinforce, and remind employees* that the mission is cost containment. Day after day, people are encouraging each other to respond to the change of priorities. Nobody has to rewrite a job description, and yet at the end of the year everyone's job description has automatically expanded and adapted to the new reality. Not only are the reviews relevant, but they can measure how individuals and groups responded to the emergency.

The reason for this is that employees who know what's important can pivot to new priorities more quickly than bureaucratic business processes can. They notice when colleagues perform and achieve important results—and reward what they "see."

Discretionary effort happens in the space between documented goals and is often more important for long-term company success because it is unshackled by the bureaucratic overhead of definition. The business world needs to make decisions quickly; employees know what's important at any given time.

> *Employees who know what's important can pivot to new priorities more quickly than bureaucratic business processes can.*

Culture is a powerful company asset, but it is also a fragile one. It must be nurtured with trust, constant reinforcement, and universal buy-in. The traditional performance review system, however, creates too many cynics today, and cynicism is poison to company culture.

Wouldn't it be great if the performance management process actually created the culture it was designed to measure? Social recognition is sometimes viewed as a measurement system. You can look at the analytics and see who the top performers are. By its very nature, social recognition also propagates the values themselves because it gets everybody thinking in one way. People ask, "Is that behavior linked to our values or not?"

As everyone grows into monitoring those attributes that define the culture, all participants become highly sensitive to the right values and behaviors, and the environment repeats and rewards those attributes.

What's "Strategic" About Recognition?

Strategic recognition is all about delivering on your business goals. It helps employees understand the behavioral norms you have identified that will lead to achieving the desired business outcome—and it does this for all employees in your company, regardless of where they live and work. To understand the power of this concept, it's helpful to examine those two words separately.

Strategic suggests that if you do recognition right, you will care about recognition beyond its boost to morale. A truly strategic program gives the CEO new insights into the behavioral norms and the culture that drives the company by analyzing recognition data. Appreciation will have a positive and measurable effect on productivity.[4]

Recognition in the strategic context means constant reinforcement of strategic values. For example, if quality is a corporate value, you must be able to give "quality" a rich meaning applicable to the way your employees behave every day. The recognition system does this by engaging the very real human emotions that go along with recognizing and being recognized for positive behaviors.

What if, instead of focusing on the glass paperweight with the employee's name engraved on it, recognition was about real human appreciation? What if the focus was on the special wording in the recognition moment, and the material reward was chosen later by the employee? Managers would have to drop the organizational mask and show themselves as sincerely appreciative individuals! What would that do to the company's culture?

Social recognition is a values propagation system as well as a measurement system.

The transformative power of rewarding behavior to drive values deep into an organization relies on clear and consistent communication at all levels and in every location of a company. No tool is more powerful for achieving this than strategic recognition.

Incentives Versus Recognition

An executive may respond, "What about incentives for performance? When members of my sales staff exceed their goals, they get bonus pay. When my managers perform exceptionally, they get profit-sharing (cash or stock options). We hold incentive competitions in which the top five performers get a trip to Cancún. Isn't that incentive enough?"

Yes, incentives can be effective management tools, but recognition is qualitatively different. It's not a question of whether management needs one or the other because recognition inspires a different set of psychic rewards from incentives. Table 4.1 contrasts the qualities of incentives with recognition.

Incentives	Recognition
Objective targets	Subjective behavior
Known reward (no surprise)	Unknown reward (surprise)
Known frequency	Unknown frequency
Infrequent (e.g., annual bonuses)	Frequent (every hour, every day)
Tangible reward primary, intangible reward secondary	Intangible reward primary, tangible reward secondary
Numbers-based	Values-based
Focused on elite few	Focused on many

Table 4.1 Incentives versus recognition

For example, incentives are earned based on objective targets. The reward is based on milestones agreed to in advance, almost always in terms of financial performance. For a sales executive, there's a clear numerical connection between closing the sale and getting the incentive. Most employees don't have that clear of a connection; their daily performance has a minimum requirement but no direct incentive to perform better. Recognition, on the other hand, rewards behavior based on values, culture, and other less easily quantified *but no less important* factors.

Like salary, incentives operate as a relationship between the employee and the organization, again based on financial performance. Recognition operates more as a direct relationship between the employee and his or her manager (or colleagues), and this is a critical difference. According to one aphorism, "People join organizations but leave managers." Recognition fosters a positive relationship with the boss.

With incentives, the number is the primary reward—it's all about keeping score. (Exceed the quota by 10 percent—get X reward. Exceed it by 20 percent—get 2X reward.) With recognition, the primary rewards are prestige, pride, satisfaction, and other psychological rewards that can far exceed the actual monetary value of the recognition given.

Recognition rewards behavior in real time, or soon after. Incentive requires more time between the action and the reward.

Note that recognition is not restricted to honoring intangible values. Some of the most effective recognition programs celebrate financial performance, hitting milestones, saving money, and similar goals. The key difference between incentives and recognition is recognition's connection between values and behavior.

Thus incentives and recognition coexist as different management tools that address different critical goals of the organization. We might say that incentives are about hitting targets (left brain) and that recognition is about applying values (right brain).

Two Forms of Motivation

Not all motivation is equal. Motivation can be extrinsic or intrinsic. Table 4.2 shows how the two forms of motivation compare in a workplace.

Extrinsic Motivation	Intrinsic Motivation
Rewards come from reaching preset goals	Rewards are not expected
Employees work solely for that reward	Satisfaction comes from a personal sense of achievement
Lack of reward results in demotivation	Lack of reward does not eliminate motivation
Not sustainable; causes reward inflation	Inspires creativity and out-of-the-box thinking

Table 4.2 Comparison of extrinsic versus intrinsic motivation

Purely extrinsic motivation relies on predetermined goals and predetermined rewards. Employees need constant reprompting by the reward to feel motivated.

Purely intrinsic motivation, with no reward at all, is also problematic. It can depend on people being so self-reliant and internally focused that it is disconnected from your company.

The best combination of motivators for business, therefore, is a balance of extrinsic and intrinsic motivation. An unexpected reward accompanied by public praise is the ideal solution to ensure the right motivation with the right connection.

Recognition by peers is one sign that the company's culture has spread from the elite to the majority. Colleagues at any level of an organization bond with their peers, associate with them, share their successes and their obstacles. To institute peer recognition is to empower coworkers to honor each others' achievements, which is a powerful and cohesive force. When peers recognize each others' contributions, they build trust. Silo walls fall, and information flows more freely. Recognition boosts morale while also relieving managers of the pressure of having to stay close to everyone (peers often know each other's contributions better than the boss).

> ## The Power of Positive Reinforcement
>
> Even in tough-minded cultures, positive reinforcement is a powerful driver of culture. U.S. Marine training might be strenuous and even abusive, but that initiation process is not the culture. The stress of marine boot camp serves as much to *identify* marines as it does to train them. Once established as a marine, an individual experiences profound recognition on a daily basis—reinforced by the mottos, the uniform, the unit cohesion, the intense group loyalty. Marines display recognition for their service and sacrifice on their uniforms in the form of medals, ribbons, and rank insignia. All these inspire pride and internal reward. Marine culture is intensely about recognition. Watch two retired marines in conversation—20 years after their service ended, they'll still call each other "marine."

Because this is about professional recognition, not personal popularity, peer recognition, like other kinds, requires the discipline of management practice underlying it. This is another way in which a formal recognition program contributes to better-managed departments.

Who doesn't enjoy honoring a colleague? It's empowering and builds general good feeling. When most employees participate, the company acquires a precious asset: a companywide culture of appreciation.

Recognition also serves as an early warning system in a large organization because it tracks optimum performance. When recognition is continuously tracked by management and executives, it reveals discrepancies and disconnects between managers and their staffs. For example, if recognition is not happening in a department, that's an early signal that something's going wrong. Is performance substandard? Is the manager unable to notice or reward the right behaviors and outcomes? Conversely, what if a department is performing magnificently but the manager is not recognizing or rewarding employees? That points to a potential risk of losing employees or to a manager who is out of touch.

Using company values as the reason for recognition also allows management to track understanding of these values by individual, team, division, region, or the company as a whole. For example, if the value of teamwork is measured across divisions and one division is found to be well behind others in its acts of teamwork, then management can target intervention in the form of additional training, mentoring from other divisions, and the like, all focused on increasing teamwork.

The Recognition Moment

To show how social recognition creates a practice of lifelogging the company, here is a short preview of recognition in action. (We get into greater detail in Chapters 6–8.)

For the purpose of managing performance, you can think of an employee's behavior in the workplace as a continuous stream of interactions with information and with others. The "crowd" whose opinion we are seeking to capture is everyone who interacts with that person. When someone in the crowd sees someone take an action that is worthy of praise and notice, he or she shows appreciation, notes the action in a durable record, and says why it is significant. That's a *recognition moment.*

Saying "thank you" is positive but not sufficient to magnify the impact of the action. The action should be recognized publicly and be connected to a specific event or behavior in a detailed way and to a value of the culture, as shown in Figure 4.1.

As shown in the figure, the system has logged a peer-to-peer recognition moment. One employee has noted and thanked another for innovation, enthusiasm, and leadership on a specific project. (Since everyone participates in recognition, this could also log a manager-to-employee moment, an employee-to-executive moment, or an interdepartmental moment.)

Other peers from the crowd can join in, as shown in Figure 4.2.

The recognition is accompanied by a tangible reward that amplifies the recognition moment, as research consistently shows.

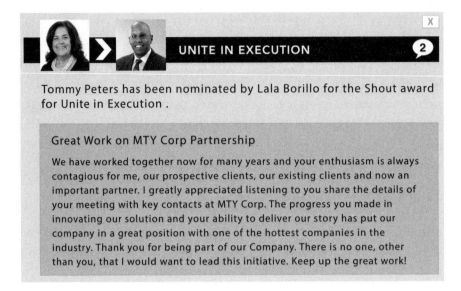

Figure 4.1 The initial recognition moment

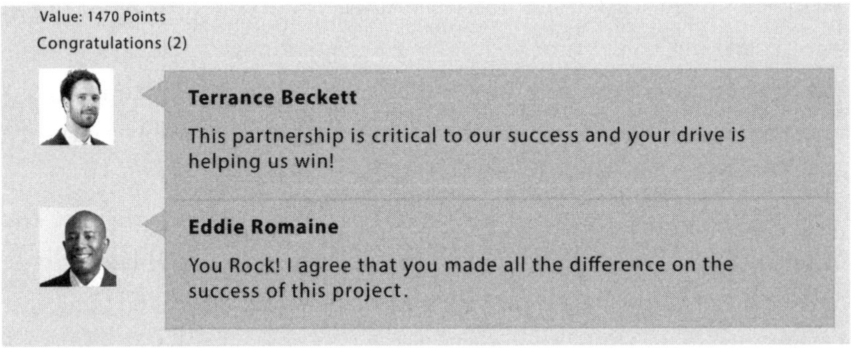

Figure 4.2 Recognition magnified by the "crowd" of other employees

Note that a recognition moment takes place in real time, close to the event or behavior that inspired it. Memory is fresh, and someone has committed his or her time to record the event, the reason it's significant, and the company value it illustrates. Placed into a database, this moment and any others concerning an employee can be retrieved and considered.

The traditional performance review is an annual, one-day sit-down with one person for a forced interaction about performance. The responsibility for recording these moments belongs entirely to the person conducting the review. Contrast this to a social recognition environment, in which recording special moments is delegated to a crowd, rather than to a single manager and a single employee.

An employee can sit down several times a year with his or her manager and retrieve the discretionary effort instances that the crowd has recorded. They can have a high-quality conversation about real-life instances in which the employee exhibited great discretionary effort, which is high performance. In effect, the crowd is in the room with the manager and the employee, contributing to the performance dialogue.

Tips for Praising and Appreciating Employees Successfully

- *Give specific praise that goes far beyond a generic "Great job!" to make recognition truly meaningful.* With specific praise, you tell the recipients what they did, how that behavior/effort reflected the company values, and why it was important to the team/department/company or contributed to achieving strategic objectives.
- *Praise actions that you want to see repeated.* By giving employees such specific recognition, you clearly communicate what is important and encourage them to repeat those actions in the future. For employees to want to repeat such desired behaviors, however, you must . . .
- *Make the praise and recognition authentic.* Don't fall into the compliment sandwich trap by saying things like, "Great job on that task, but you forgot this one critical step. I know you'll get it next time, since you are so conscientious!" This is a confusing message to employees. Did they really do a good job if an important step was missed? Offer constructive criticism, which is also desired by employees, separately from praise for work well done.

Three Trends to Watch

Three leading-edge trends in recognition are connected to performance management using the wisdom of crowds. Two have fascinating implications; one is fraught with difficulties.

Gamification

Put together an online crowd, an objective, some rules and rewards, and you have a game. In the last few years the popularity of massive multi-player (MMP) games like Farmville and other Facebook-based competitions have led designers to apply their interactive game mechanisms to crowdsourced problem solving. To cite one example, scientists at the University of Washington used an online game called Foldit to discover the structure of an enzyme from an HIV-like virus. In ten days, 46,000 players participated in a "cooperative competition" that solved a problem that had eluded scientists for 15 years![5]

I've seen several attempts at gamification of recognition systems, in which all participants get some level of scoring or status based on how often they participate. Gamification is intended to increase participation by making recognition more fun and by rewarding the participants. Gamification is ideal for taking tasks and making them more appealing by inserting a competitive element. The game attempts to inspire greater inclination toward this action. Clearly, this isn't needed for recognition given that it's something people want to naturally do!

Some elements of gamification are important and useful and can add real value to recognition. For example, according to the Incentive Research Foundation, designers are using game mechanics to customize the gaming experience so that it is mapped directly to the "capabilities and unique skills of those playing."[6] This could indeed make participation easier and even more fun. It has great promise for remote employees and work-at-home people or telecommuters.

But a number of case studies show us that today gamification of this sort tempts people to subvert the integrity of the system. You nominate me, and I can get a better review, and then I nominate you, and you'll get a better review. That's nothing less than people colluding against the company, which just poisons the culture.

More promising are the feedback mechanisms that are emerging from online game design. What if each employee could check his or her recognition profile to monitor progress in a particular skill or habit? What if a crowdsourced social recognition program could work together with a personal "worklogging" system to show what work had impact on others in real time? What if the combined data could be visualized to show, instantly and over time, the result of different sets of actions? This feedback could function as a tireless "personal effectiveness coach" for each employee.

Badging

Badging is a visible representation (in the form of a badge) of a gamified system that is rewarding certain behaviors. When this is applied to the core actions (nominate/receive) of a recognition program, it can cause trouble.

Suppose that Cindy nominates a lot of people for awards. She's on the alert for good work, and she's putting in voluntary effort to recognize others. So far, so good. But what if she had an incentive beyond her voluntary participation? Perhaps the system gives her a badge as a "top nominator" and even gives her a monetary reward when she makes 20 nominations.

That kind of system skews the data. Now that Cindy is tempted to recognize people for her own gain, her judgment could be clouded. Her awards are less spontaneous and perhaps less sincere. Once doubt creeps into the system, it loses legitimacy. Now Cindy's manager has to decide whether she's nominating people for her own gain, and weigh that intangible possibility as she approves the award. The system and its data have become suspect.

The rule of thumb should be anything that incentivizes award nominations beyond observed behavior should be viewed skeptically. The legitimacy of the data and the integrity of the recognition moment are crucial to reaping the added value of a social recognition program. As we will see later, systems can be built that provide great insight into the top performers, people who are at risk for leaving, top influencers, and high-performing departments and divisions. It's crucial that the source of all this insight has not been corrupted.

Game mechanics might inspire great innovations in recognition systems, but anything that compromises the motivation of a natural recognition moment should be viewed with skepticism.

Social Goals

Recently there's been a lot of speculation about "social goals" but the opacity of the term has caused confusion and, frankly, some fuzzy thinking. For decades, companies have set their macro goals (targets for sales and revenue, margin, operating income, etc.) and in a high-functioning company those proliferate through the organization so that everyone's individual goals support the big macro goal.

The misconception in current conversation is that the goals of the company should be crowdsourced so that at the grassroots level each employee will create his or her own goals for the coming year, and (claim the proponents) the sum of those goals is a more efficient way of goal-setting because people know what they can do better than the leadership of a big company. Goals should bubble up from the bottom, goes the thinking.

Unfortunately, that interpretation simply repeats the problem in the opposite direction. The line manager and team employee can't assemble a coordinated strategy addressing shareholder obligations, global opportunities, legal restrictions, strategic concerns, and the other issues that executive leadership faces. In a well-performing company macro goals are set to satisfy a constellation of stakeholders and to address opportunities and threats based on public and private information. Smart executives get the right information continuously from the frontline employees (and government, the board of directors, etc.), and communicate strategy continuously throughout the company.

Social goals belong in an iterative process in which leadership sets the macro targets, and the execution of those goals is delegated and split and organized to reach the right people at the grassroots level. That's the traditional, logical path. In the social goals environment, the next step is that people get to collaborate with their peers to organize the execution of those goals. In a high-performing company, employees set their own goals with a thorough understanding of how they relate to the overall goal. This is the source of much innovation, creativity, and autonomy.

> *In a knowledge economy, almost all work is collaborative, that is, social.*

In a knowledge economy, almost all work is collaborative, that is, social. Take the example of a public relations specialist preparing a press release about a new product: He or she has to get content from product management, sales, marketing, and others. Without that input, the press release can't be written. In a social goals environment, the PR professional actually gives the provision of content to each of those other professionals upon whom he or she depends, and they must accept or reject that goal as part of their job. Accepted, that socially generated goal now belongs to that peer in product management or sales or wherever. This formalizes the interdependence of modern work and creates a more reality-based set of goals. Rejected, that socially generated goal reveals a flaw in the system (public relations can't do its job) or becomes part of a negotiation in job goals. For example, a sales director might negotiate goals for one of the managers to include giving PR the content it needs. What succeeded or failed informally in the past, and was typically invisible, now becomes visible and part of someone's job.

Seen this way, social goals mean communication and collaboration among interdependent disciplines in setting detailed performance goals.

5

The Business Case for Crowdsourcing

"Culture is king," said Trevor. Rebecca smiled, and he added, "I guess I always say that."

"Yes, you do," said Rebecca. "And you're right. How does it feel to back up that statement with data, at last?"

"Feels good," he replied. "Feels even better when I look at the monthly financials and see you're under budget for recruiting this year."

"Savings are mostly from decreased turnover in the core business. It's down 30 percent year-over-year. The real test will come when the GeoClean acquisition goes through. We lost 25 percent of the people from the last company we brought on."

"That many?" said Trevor.

"The 30 percent includes severance packages, but the voluntary quits alone hit us with a lot of replacement costs, not to mention the lost talent."

Trevor asked, "What do you project for attrition this time?"

Rebecca answered, "The mergers group and I are setting a target of 15 percent, including severance. GeoClean's a lean company, which is good for us, but more to the point, I think getting everyone integrated with the social recognition system right away will help us establish ties between Hydrolab and GeoClean employees. I want to take some of our recruitment savings and put it toward a social integration and on-boarding task force to make that happen."

Joanna Geraghty of JetBlue has a unique challenge when it comes to creating a Positivity Dominated Workplace. Using JetBlue's terms crewmembers (employees) and crewleaders (managers), she poses the situation: "Our pilots and inflight crewmembers do not come to an office. They come in, they check their schedule, and they leave. In a business like ours where crewleaders can go months without seeing crewmembers face to face, recognition absolutely plays a special role. You do not want the only touch point the crewleader has with a crewmember to be a negative touch point. So how do you create opportunities for positive touch points, particularly when you have a remote workforce?"[1]

Joanna continues with the importance of a consistent workplace narrative: "When you operate a flight, whether it is the ground handlers loading the baggage or the airport crewmembers boarding customers, whether it is the captain and first officer flying the plane, or the mechanic ensuring that everything is in order prior to departure, whether it is the in-flight crewmember delivering a great onboard experience, it is truly a team approach. So when you can recognize somebody on the team for doing a great job, it is pretty special."

Joanna concludes by sharing, "One of the things we love to do at JetBlue is tell stories, and one pilot epitomized that positive workplace narrative when he wrote this: 'As your Captain, it is a pleasure to have you on my crew since you always go above and beyond for our customers while always being there for your fellow crewmembers, too. I saw the face on the couple that did not understand English relax and calm down with your actions. I saw the kid's eyes go from tears to a smile. You do it in such a way that is second nature. I hope you don't mind getting a pat on the back because your actions deserve this and much more.'"[2]

The modern company is a social enterprise, and it is changing with the cultural shifts brought about by social media and social networking.

Recent Changes in Work and the Workplace

First, let's examine some of the ways our work and workplaces have changed in the last decade.

Change 1: Companies Become More Like Communities

Large companies are like cities.[3] People belong to defined communities, communicate about shared work or play, operate in a complex set of social rules and traditions, and cooperate or compete depending on their interests. The population is multigenerational and diverse, and social circles, whether defined by work structures like a department or informal constructs like a shared interest in technology, set the most visible boundaries of communication. This has been true for a long time. What's different today is how members of communities interact.

Companies like IBM, GE, or Citigroup have long operated in global clusters bounded by geography and work discipline. Future leaders are rotated among locations and business lines to broaden their experience and also to broaden their professional networks, because social capital in the form of trusted relationships between leaders is crucial to effectiveness in the present and in the future. In big organizations, centers of opportunity such as growing business lines, innovation centers, and high-profile departments are the proving ground for talent and the nurturing ground of strong relationships. Backwaters and underperforming areas also exist (and potential leaders are often sent to fix them). Across this complex social system, top performers and average employees interact daily. They observe one another's behavior, form opinions about each other, and develop reputations among communities.

The social structure of a company can be read as a story that is both a history—"our founding, our growth, our future"—and a cultural tip sheet—"our values, and why we did/do things a particular way." Great business leaders cite the story for exactly the same reasons political leaders cite national history—to link the present and future to the past, to reinforce values, and to give a larger meaning to today's work. Companies like IBM stand for something, even when the story has grim passages (as when IBM had a near-death experience in the 1990s and reinvented itself as a services, consulting, and "solutions" business).

The story builds affinity, shared purpose, and community among different members. Initiatives are built around its principles. For example, IBM's Corporate Service Corps is a program that enlists high-potential young employees to spend time solving information technology problems in third-world countries. It is highly competitive: In its first year 100 members were selected from 5,500 applicants. It focuses on IBM's core business of technology consulting but broadens the scope for social good. It is international and diverse. Members of the corps train together and develop strong long-term business relationships. IBM's Corporate Service Corps contributes to many narrative and cultural threads in the company's story, and that's more than just a public relations effort.[4]

The story might be inspired and spread by leadership, but it becomes part of the culture only when the community at large retells it. People reinforce and spread the values when they share the story, and this happens in interactions as diverse as happy-hour conversations and messages of congratulations.

The story is also the foundation of the company's employer brand, the sum total of reasons that people want to work there. HR executives know that an authentic employer brand is a great value proposition for potential hires and inside the company for building and maintaining morale.

Change 2: Work Moves from Synchronous to Asynchronous

As we saw in Chapter 1, the move from synchronous to asynchronous information flow means that even the most complex products can be dismantled into constituent parts that can be assembled in a number of potential sequences, and this disrupts long-standing work routines. Crowdsourcing software development, for example in the open-source operating system Linux, is the apotheosis of this asynchronous work. Similarly, the flexible supply chain systems developed in recent years continuously adapt to changes in delivery schedules by making sequenced delivery of parts or components less important.

Synchronous work means that you first receive someone's action, and then you perform a corresponding action. With a low information flow, such as dealing with the postal mail in an office circa 1970, that is simple. Even if the system speeds up, as when e-mail replaced postal mail, the sequence remained.

Have you caught yourself saying, "This week I'm going to clear out my e-mail. I'm going to catch up on reading my Twitter feed. I'm going to look through all those pictures on Instagram, and I'm going to respond to all those friend requests and messages on Facebook." That would be an unbelievable amount of work, and by next week you'd be back in the same situation.

This information tsunami cannot be managed sequentially or in a synchronous, time-bound method. Instead, we have created queuing systems for actions. Information comes in and instantly gets prioritized. Managing one's own work increasingly means moving from synchronous patterns (action $\rightarrow$ reaction) to asynchronous patterns (action $\rightarrow$ queue $\rightarrow$ search/prioritize $\rightarrow$ reaction).

Some of the information is trivial, but much of it is highly valuable. The trouble arises in the fact that it's all sent (via e-mail, feeds, LinkedIn, etc.) in an asynchronous stream, and we have to impose order on it so that we can act efficiently to separate the straw from the gold. Since we cannot command the world to send us information in the most efficient sequence, we adapt to manage the stream.

Now let's look at this from a performance management perspective. An ideal performance management system would capture all the behaviors and decisions of an employee in a kind of stream (asynchronous action) and sort through that information, finding the gold. The most valuable actions would be highlighted, recognized, and retrievable in some recorded form. These would become "priority behaviors" similar to the valuable information in the queue above. Indeed, a record of priority behaviors might be the most valuable information that comes to a manager's notice. With these records, a manager could reinforce, encourage, and prioritize the highest-value behaviors. A manager could propagate those behaviors throughout the organization by offering them up as examples. In human learning, observation and example are the clearest form of learning and teaching behavior.

> *The most valuable actions should be recognized, recorded, and retrievable.*

These work behaviors don't happen in a straight-line, synchronous pattern, however. Machines long ago replaced human beings in doing synchronous, repetitive tasks, and today's work requires constant adjustments, large and small, to the situation at hand. Work involving judgment, decision making, problem solving, learning, and communication is inherently asynchronous. Information technology is required to capture the golden moments in a nonlinear work environment.

Change 3: Work Moves from Location-Specific to Location-Neutral

Location is another big structural change taking place today, as the popularity of smart mobile devices makes any place with a wireless Internet connection a potential workplace. This has been familiar for a decade since the BlackBerry became the first widely used e-mail-handling device, but we've recently taken leaps past e-mail as tablets and even smartphones access the power of cloud computing environments. Employees can consume information and act on it anytime, anywhere. Cloud storage means that many people can work simultaneously on a project from anywhere on the planet. Instant communication has the quality of conversation and informal exchange, which is different from formal communication in long documents or e-mails.

The portion of work that is accomplished within a central work site is shrinking, and the portion of work accomplished anywhere else is growing. This has implications for performance reviews. "Face time" is less important than actual quality and quantity of work, and collaboration is organized by technology, not centralized in a workplace. As social technologies like Quora, Facebook, and Twitter encourage long-range collaboration even brainstorming doesn't have to be done face to face.

As a result, an individual's performance is observed among far-flung collaborators, not just his or her manager and work site peers. As face time becomes less critical for getting work done, a fair and accurate performance management system has to collect observations from the crowd of collaborators and measure work according to results, not attendance or popularity.

A Less Discriminatory Environment?

The rise of asynchronous work collaboration is an interesting development in terms of making objective opinions of performance, without interference of race, age, gender, nationality, and other distinguishing characteristics. As visual cues diminish in work communication, I wonder if prejudice in performance reviews will decline. People who are part of each other's social circles might simply not meet until after they have a firm impression. If "C. J." in your mind's eye is a young man, will your impression change when you discover she's a middle-aged woman? Might your judgment of someone's performance be cleared of subtle prejudice? Studies tell us, for example, that people form negative impressions about overweight employees,[5] but what if you don't learn this about someone until long after you know his performance based on discretionary effort and actual results?

Change 4: Horizontal Loyalty Replaces Vertical Loyalty

More than a decade ago, Dan Pink observed in his book *Free Agent Nation*[6] the growing free agent mindset among permanent workers, in which a job is viewed more as a temporary contract than a lifelong relationship with a company. The free agent mindset favored work relationships on a peer basis, which he called horizontal loyalty, as opposed to the more traditional bond between manager and managed (dubbed vertical loyalty).

Pink observed that employees now have less security in the form of a permanent job but more in the form of a reputation in the larger community of potential clients and employers. The wider the reputation, the greater its value because a professional community is the best source of work for a free agent (and a strong reputation means better market value such as a higher salary).

With the advent of social recognition, horizontal loyalty goes to any community that recognizes your work. Reputation management is no longer a simple matter of "managing up" or becoming the boss's favorite, but about cultivating a continuous positive conversation with the community. The "single point of failure" flaw in the traditional performance review that we saw in Chapter 1 can be overcome by workers actively managing their reputations among their peers, internal clients, coworkers, and even customers.

A Culture of Recognition

Social recognition cultivates a culture of recognition among employees, management, and executive leadership. That in turn can both define and reinforce the company culture. Since we're recommending exactly this, let's briefly consider what a long-term culture of recognition, as opposed to single recognition moments, might mean for a business.

If an employee is doing the right thing, it will be noticed, honored, and appreciated (as well as rewarded in tangible ways). This expectation motivates each person to consider what behaviors will earn that recognition, just as an expectation of promotion causes some to perform beyond their job description, or seek new skills, or take on challenging new projects. The culture of recognition can be the uniting force across the inevitable "silos" and departmental cultures in the organization.

A culture of recognition also aids in the creation of a robust social architecture in which communication flows freely, consistently, and constantly. Employees are universally encouraged to do their best—they are not just complimented, but also positively acknowledged when their behavior is aligned to company values and strategic objectives. In a multinational company, the real differences among countries and national cultures are celebrated with a global language of appreciation. It overcomes the alienation and inadvertent miscommunication that is the hobgoblin of a multinational enterprise. It encourages trust and that almost mythical bonding that soldiers call "unit cohesion."

Recognition and Management Science

When individual recognition moments across the enterprise are recorded, analyzed, and understood, recognition becomes as potent a management tool as financial- or program-management practices.

Executive Insight

High-performance cultures are shaped around the following three components:

1. **A clear, compelling corporate mission.** A statement that answers the question of why the company exists.
2. **Shared organizational values.** Core values guide employee behavior and influence business practices. Your business strategies shift to meet market demands—your core values don't.
3. **Shared accountability.** High-performance cultures require an environment that encourages employee ownership of both the organization's bottom-line results and its cultural foundation.

—Fraser Marlow, Vice President, Research and Marketing, Blessing White[7]

Strategic recognition adds the ultimate layer of value, which is culture management. Strategic recognition is linked to strategic goals such as engagement, employee satisfaction, or cultural change. But also, because you have those tools, you get to then use strategic recognition to manage the culture. In other words, you can emphasize a single value that you feel hasn't gotten the traction you need to meet your strategic objectives.

Your sales strategy doesn't focus exclusively on the moment a sales transaction closes (at least, it shouldn't). Strategic sales practices track and analyze customer relationships, planning, product development, marketing intelligence, follow-through, and growing skills of the sales staff. In the same way, strategic culture management needs a long-term plan and a set of processes to embed values and enhance the culture. Strategic and social recognition provide the foundation to affect culture over the long term.

Strategic recognition takes its place with the other "hard" management science practices. It has measurable processes. It is fully integrated into strategic planning and global resource management. Self-sustaining social and strategic recognition can bring certain values to the surface and drive a culture in which behaviors reflect organizational values and contribute to company success.

Strategic recognition aligns company culture with geographic, national, and even demographic cultures. The company's most important values are understood by everyone: young Europeans and older Asians, jocks in the financial planning department, hipster designers in marketing, and minivan-driving soccer parents in the call center. Social recognition becomes so much more than the relationship between manager and employee—it becomes the affirmation of belonging to the society we call a corporation.

Recognition Supports Two Kinds of Cultures

Executives address strategic issues. In terms of employee performance, the big strategic issues they face are building the right inward-facing (employee) culture, building the right outward-facing (customer) culture, and fostering employee engagement.

We know that culture matters—study after study demonstrates and CEO after CEO admits that an enduring culture is the only sustainable competitive advantage. Because executives are trained to trust data and deal with them all day long, organizational culture must be measured and quantified. After all, culture is a critical contributor to financial performance and every other measure of success. Once this was a radical view of a few HR visionaries. Now even the most mainstream business leaders talk openly about measuring values and culture, and researchers and management thinkers test and refine models for measuring culture all the time.

The object of *inward-facing culture* is united execution. All organizations are simply people united by common goals; employees need to work together to achieve those goals. Even with shared values and great enthusiasm, a team that is not united in its efforts is dysfunctional. Once individuals unite as a team, functioning together to achieve departmental, divisional, and company goals, they can reinforce both values and engagement. Mutual dependence develops trust, encourages learning, and fosters the sense of belonging to something greater than oneself.

As Jim Collins and his collaborators have documented in bestsellers like *Built to Last* and *Good to Great*,[8] many different sets of cultural values can lead to success. A company can value competition and thrive on change or value cooperation and thrive on consistency. What matters is the authenticity, clarity, and reinforcement of values up and down the organization, between management and managed, and among peers.

Management and, indeed, the culture itself must encourage united execution by directly rewarding it and by demonstrating its importance. That's as simple as a director instructing her managers, "Recognize all the good behavior you can, because I can't be everywhere." In a consistent culture, this is manifest in a thousand person-to-person moments, connecting the value of teamwork to specific behaviors in direct, personal, and individual recognition moments.

The object of *outward-facing culture* is a consistent and positive customer experience, aligned with the company's values and promise. Executives speak of a "brand experience" that can be repeated across product lines and customer segments.

> *The object of* inward-facing culture *is united execution.*
> *The object of* outward-facing culture *is a consistent and*
> *positive customer experience.*

Lori Gaytan of IHG (Intercontinental Hotels Group) cites the company's core purpose as delivering "Great Hotels Guests Love," a simple brand statement that can be expressed in any action by the 375,000 employees who work at IHG's corporate offices or for any of its nine hotel brands, from creating and designing a new wellness hotel brand concept like EVEN Hotels to serving dinner at a Crowne Plaza hotel downtown to checking in a guest at a Holiday Inn on Route 44. Behavior will be different, but the brand promise and the goal remain the same. Gaytan expresses the consistency of culture management when she says, "We believe how we treat our employees is how our employees will treat our guests. . . . Employees who are recognized and rewarded for their efforts feel more connected, as they truly understand the value they deliver to the business."

In a business like hospitality, employee behavior can go unobserved by managers. Performance can be recorded by feedback from the guests and from peers. Above any details of a job description, an IHG manager needs to know, "Did this employee help create a great hotel guests love?" Simple questions like that are often the most powerful.

Engaged employees create a living, robust company culture, and the height of that state is a workplace mindset I call a culture of recognition.

Recognition Drives Engagement

Engagement is the HR buzzword of the decade. Engaged employees are enthusiastic and involved; they are personally invested in better performance. Engagement suggests doing more than the job requires; it also implies that the urge to do more comes from within, as opposed to "just following orders." Discretionary effort is the heart of engagement.

Executives desire it, consultancies specialize in it, and more than 100 rigorous studies assert employee engagement's positive effect on the bottom line.[9] For example, a study by Towers Watson documented that, "Companies with higher employee engagement outperform those with lower employee engagement, relative to industry benchmarks," like revenue growth, cost of goods sold, and customer focus. Among 40 multinational companies, Towers Watson found higher operating margins and net profit margins in the firms with more engaged employees. In a book describing the insights of those studies, Towers Watson's Julie Gebauer wrote, "We consistently found that organizations and managers get the best from employees when they do five things well: know them, grow them, inspire them, involve them, and reward them. When these five principles are at the core of the work experience, there's no doubt that employees consistently give value-adding discretionary effort—and that directly impacts the organization's financial results."[10]

All studies on engagement build a consistent case that engaged employees are more productive, more focused on customers and company values, and drive better financial performance than nonengaged workers. They do higher-quality work, are safer, and are less likely to quit a job—and exhibit all these competitive advantages over nonengaged employees by double-digit margins.[11]

While there are many ways to inspire engagement (and even more to kill it), all involve communicating and rewarding desired behaviors based on defined values.

In the book *12: The Elements of Great Managing,* the Gallup organization identified 12 elements of engagement and published them as statements that employees agreed with, such as, "At work, I have the opportunity to do what I do best every day"; "In the last seven days, I have received recognition or praise for doing good work"; and "At work, my opinions seem to count." It's noteworthy that only one of the twelve statements explicitly mentions a supervisor, yet six mention encouragement from, attention from, and affinity with a fellow employee or simply "someone at work." It appears that engagement is a group effort![12]

Research Insight

Transactional Versus Emotional Engagement

A 2012 study published by the Chartered Institute of Personnel and Development (CIPD) established two types of engagement:

1. *Transactional engagement* happens when employees are happily focused on a job or task they like. It is tied to rewards like cash rewards and incentive pay, and these employees are "less likely to perform well and will quickly leave for a better offer."
2. *Emotional engagement* happens when employees have made strong ties to their bosses, coworkers, and company values. This engagement is more closely tied to public appreciation and congratulations, and these employees will do more for the organization than is normally expected because they receive "a greater and more fulfilling psychological contract."[13]

Behind the rigorous studies of engagement lies the commonsense knowledge that engaged employees perform better. But again, the purpose of performance management is to know both why and how they perform better. Crowdsourcing a profile of an engaged employee provides those details because other employees record behaviors that create value, and an engaged, energetic person models the right behaviors for others. "Watch Paula—she really knows how to treat a customer," is common advice for a manager to give a new employee because it works. If everybody is watching

Executive Insight

"Employees who believe that management is concerned about them as a whole person—not just an employee—are more productive, more satisfied, more fulfilled. Satisfied employees mean satisfied customers, which leads to profitability."

—Anne M. Mulcahy, former CEO of Xerox

Paula—and Joachim and Taylor and every other outstanding employee—the right performance gets modeled in specific behaviors.

How important is engagement to the individual? One of the top reasons people leave their current employer is the feeling that they don't count, that their work was not recognized. "I wasn't valued. My contributions weren't appreciated," are the common complaints. This leads to disaffection and alienation—the psychic opposite of engagement.

Lately, studies have focused on employee energy, which might be called Engagement 2.0. Energy is that buzz you feel when you enter a workplace full of engaged employees. It's not just discretionary effort, but *lots* of effort, an internal drive in each employee to move forward and get things done. This is actually an elusive mindset and has been variously called "flow" or "being in the zone." HR professionals, contemplating a candidate for a position, call it the difference between "can do" and "will do."

In physics, energy is the capacity to do work. Energy has two states: potential energy, stored up and accessible but motionless, and kinetic energy, released and causing something to move. So how does a leader turn the potential energy of a suboptimal workplace into the kinetic energy of a workplace full of action?

A leader has to provide good direction (where will the energy go?), purpose (the kick that starts things moving), the right environment (the tools and techniques to accomplish work), and a sense of progress (the self-renewing cycle of kinetic energy causing more energy to be released). We've seen that these are necessary conditions for an engaged workforce, and there's one more condition.

Mercer Consulting cites the critical presence of a sense of urgency in an energized workplace. Urgency is created at an individual work group and departmental level and is reinforced by colleagues and line managers on a repeated, ongoing basis. Statements of urgency from the CEO set the scene but aren't enough to sustain high levels of energy.

Ultimately, to paraphrase the political truism, "All energy is local." You are energized by yourself, your manager, and your peers, and everyone has the capacity to amplify or diminish that sense of urgency among his or her group.

Recognition Supports the Work of HR

Human resources departments manage the performance review process. They must implement a system that promotes company values and financial goals, fosters a strong company culture, is both efficient and fair, and identifies the best-performing, highest-potential employees.

They must also train managers to administer performance reviews well despite the perennial problem that most managers are not put into their position because they are excellent at giving performance reviews. This is why managers are potentially the single point of failure in performance management that we saw in Chapter 1.

If building and maintaining company culture is everybody's business—and it is—a crowdsourced performance review system is the enabling technology that makes everyone able to contribute.

Here's how social recognition contributes to the responsibilities mentioned previously:

- *It promotes company values.* Social recognition moments (when done strategically) are always connected to specific company values. As employees note one another's positive acts and connect them to values like safety or customer focus, both giver and receiver communicate the importance of particular values.

- *It promotes financial goals.* Crowdsourced feedback in the form of social recognition encourages behavior that results directly in better financial performance (money earned or saved) and behavior that results indirectly in better financial performance, for example, when someone streamlines a process to make it more efficient.
- *It fosters a strong company culture.* Culture is more than values. It is the way people behave day in, day out. Social recognition gives everyone an incentive to get in the game and power the culture.
- *It creates better efficiency.* Managers resist a performance review process that is either burdensome or takes too much time from other, urgent responsibilities. At best, managers will soldier through an inefficient process, but too often they are tempted to rush the work. At worst, they become caught in the extreme structures described in Chapter 1 and subvert the entire intention of performance management. By contrast, social recognition adds a layer of information with little effort on the part of the manager, thus providing abundant new data on which to judge performance.
- *It enhances fairness.* Above all, performance reviews must be perceived as fair. Crowdsourced performance reviews are democratic; everyone with whom a person works can register his or her (positive) experiences. The wisdom of crowds is impartial and fair by its very nature.
- *It identifies the best-performing, highest-potential employees.* Crowdsourced recognition data aggregate to show a manager both who is doing things right and outcomes like the positive impact an action has on others, on processes, and on profits. Over time, the data show who is performing at a high level consistently.
- *It promotes individual initiative.* Deliberate individual decisions, not happenstance, create a high-performance culture.

Fairmont Hotels & Resorts, a splendid example of effective hiring, spends a lot of time and money during its hiring process to identify and confirm a candidate's dedication to outstanding service. Fairmont looks for employees who want to delight hotel guests. This requires hard-to-measure qualities like empathy, creativity, and spontaneity. Matt Smith, Fairmont's vice president of human resources, EMEA & Asia Pacific, gives this example of a successful hire: "We had guests staying with us in one of our resorts in the Rocky Mountains in a room that had a big stone fireplace. As they left the room to go swimming, one of their children said, 'Mom, I can't believe there's a fireplace. Do you think they'll know how much I love marshmallows? Could we roast marshmallows?' Well, a room attendant—the person cleaning the room—happened to overhear that conversation. When the guests returned, they found a basket of marshmallows, graham crackers, and chocolates, all to make s'mores around the fire. On the basket was a little handwritten note from the employee saying, 'Because we know how much you like marshmallows.'"

"You can't engineer that kind of creativity," adds Matt. "You can't write a manual that says, 'If you ever have a kid and a fireplace, send marshmallows.' What you can do is recognize the magic that spontaneous, creative service creates, and keep hiring people who want to make that magic. And you can manage a continuous process of turning those unpredictable moments into organizational culture, through appreciation, communication, and celebration of those acts."

Recognition Supports HR Budgets

Several of these issues also have significant impact on HR budgets. A recent study by the Boston Consulting Group discovered that market-leading companies (those with double the revenue growth and profit margins of less successful firms in the same business) demonstrate excellence in developing leadership, in performance management and rewards, and in improving employer branding. To HR, this means a better return on dollars which can be invested in recruiting, training, and developing employees.[15]

Turnover is a budget-killer for HR because the cost of replacing employees who quit ranges from 50 percent to 150 percent of a year's salary.[17] Lack of recognition for a job well done is the second most common reason people quit (after compensation).[18] The 48.3 percent of voluntary

Are You Missing Your Influencers?

"One of the most powerful and innovative aspects of a social recognition platform is the data it yields," says Tom Aurelio, vice president, global human resources at Symantec. "Recognition data allows managers to see who their top performers are, monitor individual and departmental interaction, and use peer-to-peer recognition data to provide a new viewpoint into employee performance. As an HR leader, I now have actionable data. Executives can finally sit down and figure out who our influencers are throughout the business."[16]

departures that cited lack of recognition represent a preventable turnover cost. Crowdsourcing performance management decreases turnover by increasing recognition and improving morale.

Let's do the math: A company with 10,000 employees with an average salary/benefit package of $40,000 spends $400 million directly on people. An 11 percent turnover rate incurs a replacement cost of more than $41 million. (See Figure 5.1.) Even if all your employees were entry-level workers making $8 an hour, your annual turnover cost would be more than $3 million. And that doesn't even begin to account for the brain drain, opportunity cost, and risks associated with losing valuable social knowledge and talent. (HR execs: Feel free to do this simple math with your company's turnover and salary numbers.)

Good human resources practices create virtuous cycles, self-sustaining cascades of cause and effect that promote good work across many dimensions of a workplace. It's this that enables social recognition, and the crowdsourced performance review, to create value beyond the obvious return on investment. By making a company a better place to work, social recognition and improved performance management make the company more attractive to the best and brightest candidates, which in turn improves performance, which in turn improves morale, which

CALCULATING TURNOVER COSTS

We profiled a sample company of 10,000 employees with a very conservative 11% annual turnover rate and an average cost to replace of 75%

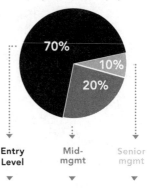

Company with 10,000 Employees

70% 10% 20%

Entry Level   Mid-mgmt   Senior mgmt

Average Annual Salaries

$30K $70K $150K

Cost to Replace (@75% of salary)

$22.5K $52.5K $112.5K

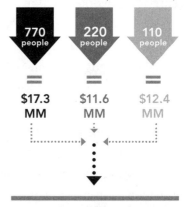

Annual Loss of Talent (@11% turnover)

770 people   220 people   110 people

= $17.3 MM   = $11.6 MM   = $12.4 MM

$41.3MM

in bottom-line turnover costs

Figure 5.1

makes the company an even better place to work. For HR executives, the crowdsourcing of performance management improves the state of the company well beyond its quantifiable return on investment.

Tom Aurelio of Symantec believes that social recognition makes budget spending more effective. "One of the great advantages of this tool is we can really monitor how much of our reward and recognition dollars are going towards each value," Aurelio explains. "We have not been able to do that in the past. And it has really helped us drive our business results."[19]

Crowdsourced Feedback Deepens the Dialogue

The manager's case for a crowdsourced performance review reflects his or her frontline position. Because management is the practice of achieving work through others and of leading and evaluating the progress of a group, managers hold the primary responsibility for improving the performance of the group and its members. Whether this is a manager leading ten people at a shipping center or a general manager leading 30 department managers in a 5,000-employee division, accountability for improving performance lies at any level with the person in charge.

Crowdsourced feedback and recognition offer a supplement to any style of performance review because they enrich and deepen the dia-

Executive Insight

"With our social recognition program, we're getting crowdsourced feedback into the daily behaviors and performance of our employees. It gives us greater insight and clarity into the behaviors and performance that are truly moving the business forward. This is powerful data that offers a wider set of viewpoints about employee performance and how we're living the values."

—Lori Gaytan, Senior Vice President of Human Resources at IHG (InterContinental Hotels Group)[20]

logue between managers and subordinates, whether the style is focused on competencies, quotas, projects, or coaching.

Adding crowdsourced data to the performance review via social recognition sets a positive tone sought by managers and staff alike, because reviews exist to guide and clarify performance. For the "satisfactory" or "meets expectations" employees, whose performance is fine if not stellar, social recognition points out and flags specific behaviors that are critical to improved performance. Specific behaviors allow the manager to offer concrete observations and probe the reasons for better-than-average moments in the course of an employee's work. Managers can find these moments by themselves, but cannot observe nearly as many as the crowd enabled by social recognition. The right behavior, noticed and recognized by someone on the team, can open the way to dialogue that might otherwise be missed by managers and employees.

Crowdsourced feedback and recognition improve the less pleasant task of rating an underperforming member of the team, and this should be a relief to managers. As noted in Chapter 1, 63 percent of HR executives believe that managers' lack of courage to have difficult performance discussions was the top challenge in performance management.[21] Managers frequently do not do a good job of providing feedback to less-than-impressive employees, don't provide feedback in a timely fashion, and are inconsistent in how they rate and reward behaviors.

"Lack of courage" might sound harsh concerning difficult performance discussions, but it's human nature to avoid bad news and potential conflict. Managers must base their judgments on facts. This is why, even in the case of underperforming employees, crowdsourced performance data improve the traditional review because they build an objective vision of performance, or lack of it. Managers can paint a picture of the future for employees, when colleagues and team members are rewarding and appreciating the employees' impact. The employees can then take specific actions in their daily work to have more impact on the success of their colleagues, their workplace, and the company.

Crowdsourced recognition increases the reach of a manager's core task: positive feedback. In 2009, Gallup released research that found that the feedback style of a manager can profoundly impact employee engagement.[22] Gallup said:

- Managers who focus on employee *strengths* have 61 percent engaged employees and 1 percent actively disengaged.
- Managers who focus on employee *weaknesses* have 45 percent engaged employees and 22 percent actively disengaged.
- Managers who *ignore* their employees have 2 percent engaged employees and 40 percent actively disengaged.

Employees crave any indication that what they do matters—but too many managers prefer to simply ignore the most basic of managerial duties. How many? According to Gallup, 25 percent of employees place themselves in the "ignored" category.

Basic management training always emphasizes that frequent positive feedback improves performance for the group. Multiply individual instances of discretionary effort by 10 or 20 team members, and you're building real momentum toward excellent performance across the vast majority of employees.

In a social recognition situation, many more people can add their voices of approval, and this is empowering to everyone. There are only a few ways a peer can improve the performance of a peer, and among them are offering encouragement and approval. In addition, spreading responsibility for rewarding performance in a positive program also spreads accountability for improving performance to all. The manager's accountability continues but is bolstered by empowering the wider community.

Managers might assume that only stellar performers should be recognized. If 30 percent are star players, it follows that 70 percent of workers won't get recognition. But those are invaluable people. Limiting recognition to only spectacularly performing employees limits its impact to only a select few instead of the majority of the company.

Towers Watson found that, "The key to driving productivity gains is increasing engagement among core contributors. . . . Highly engaged employees are already working at or near their peak but are often limited by their less engaged coworkers. Focusing on engaging core contributors can improve both groups' productivity." [23]

Crowdsourcing performance management among every employee breaks the psychological barrier that divides the elite from the rank and file. It expands goodwill and helps employees share enthusiasm and mutual respect.

I often hear the concern, "We won't be able to find enough positive behavior to create a significant amount of crowdsourced data." In my experience this has never been a problem. People want to excel, and the momentum of many people recognizing each other often builds on itself. People want to be recognized and feel significant; it's human nature. Holding a mirror to that remark, I ask, "Are you really telling me that you don't have enough good performance from your people to recognize it frequently?"

Adding crowdsourced data to the review of an outstanding employee enriches the dialogue as well. Managers take pleasure in reviewing the performance of the elite players, and yet the potential weakness of a review that is nonspecific still pertains. A manager might say, "Who cares how she delivered that product on time and under budget? She did it, and that's great!" That point of view implies a lost opportunity because such success deserves a thoughtful review in order to capture best practices, breakthrough moments, and inspiring behaviors.

Finally, crowdsourced performance data help managers locate those high performers who, by virtue of their position or modest temperament,

Executive Insight

"Outstanding leaders go out of their way to boost the self-esteem of their personnel. If people believe in themselves, it's amazing what they can accomplish."

—Sam Walton, founder of Walmart [24]

might otherwise go unnoticed. We've seen that the crowd judges all manner of issues more accurately than do individuals, and social recognition can spot great performers early in their careers. Managers can accelerate their development sooner than a traditional performance review would.

Voluntary Participation Is Key

The business case recommending a crowdsourced performance review from the employee's perspective is built on its democratic appeal.

Recognition moments are voluntary, and this produces beneficial effects for all. Because the power to reward good performance is distributed throughout the company, employees become accountable to one another and are energized to interact. They have a social incentive to be on the lookout for behavior that improves the bottom line, morale, or efficiency of a business unit.

Voluntary accolades are genuine. Nobody has to make the effort to recognize someone. The mere fact that someone was inspired to take the time to recognize another, to do something for nothing in return, speaks enormously well of the person who has received the award. A peer or manager could notice extra effort and just as easily let it go unrecognized. This inspirational element of volunteerism gives special legitimacy to the moment and to the crowdsourced behavioral data it produces.

Voluntary participation increases the sense of personal attachment to better performance—both for the individual and the group. Not coincidentally, it also inspires faith that the performance review system is fair because a crowdsourced review is balanced. All kinds of relationships are reflected in recognition, from a senior manager recognizing outstanding results to a distant peer saying thank you for a small favor.

When you enlist all employees in a voluntary program of noticing good behavior and rewarding it, you create a wider pool of knowledge for formal employee appraisals, succession planning, leadership development, and even flight risk assessment.

Because it depends on voluntary initiative, social recognition inspires employee engagement, which is the extra discretionary effort that HR professionals have said for the past decade is the difference between success and failure in relation to the competition.

Kevin Sheridan, in *Building a Magnetic Culture*, made the point that "engaged employees are ten times more likely to feel good work is recognized and seven times more likely to feel they receive regular performance feedback."[25]

Every employee of a company from top to bottom answers to someone. Whether the company culture is hierarchical or egalitarian, all have a stake in its success, and all are accountable to each other. Adding social recognition to the culture means that employees have a say, a positive say, in what will become of the company in the years to come. In that sense, it increases the power of each individual to make the business better.

Bottom line: A Positivity Dominated Workplace supported at all levels by social recognition is energizing to all.

PART 2 PUTTING THE CROWDSOURCED PERFORMANCE REVIEW INTO PRACTICE

6

How Recognition Supplements the Traditional Performance Review

Liz wasn't used to face time with Trevor, but he'd asked her to join Rebecca to discuss the progress of the performance management program. In the conference room, Liz connected her laptop to the projector and opened her team's social graph.

"Before you start, one question," said Trevor. "Are you confident that the social recognition program is improving performance?"

Liz replied, "It already is improving performance, in some surprising ways." She directed attention to the graph. "We were told that giving everyone a stake in the performance process would raise awareness of what actions promoted Hydrolab values, but let's face it, a bunch of software engineers need to be convinced by the evidence. What surprised me is that once they got going, the people on my team started to pay more attention to each others' work."

Liz highlighted paths in her team's social graph with a laser pointer. "What I see in this chart is everyone's ambition to notice one another's good work and remark on it. That makes the new people more secure and gets the people who have been here longer to look up from their monitors once in a while."

"So there's more communication as well as goodwill," said Trevor.

"Definitely," said Liz. "And here's something I had not anticipated: The crowdsourced performance review input will net out to less work for me at review time, not more."

"How's that?" asked Trevor.

"Twenty-two of my people this year have provided me with specific and detailed stories of good performance. I've got actual data to work with now. Instead of saying someone's performing at a 4.5 level of management based only on outcomes, I get an actual narrative about what they do and how they do it." Liz clicked on a young woman's picture and the screen changed. "Take a look at this report on Dana Santori. I'm putting her forward for the Geo-Clean integration project."

Adding crowdsourced performance data through social recognition is a deliberately simple process. Chapter 1 concluded with a complete list of ways social recognition fixes the traditional review. Here's a shortened version of that list, focusing on the operational needs of the traditional review.

Social recognition must:

- Fix the "single point of failure" problem
- Preserve managers' accountability
- Make performance objectives adapt to changing business conditions
- Give detailed performance data on individuals, teams, and departments
- Include hard-to-quantify factors like creativity

Traditional performance reviews differ in scope, format, length, and complexity. One company might be happy with a 1–5 scale of performance, another might favor the 360-degree technique, a third company might focus entirely on objectives, and another might swear by the competency-based review. There are plenty of models and vendors to choose from; all have trade-offs and advantages, and they also have much in common. For example, reviews tend to be useful for aiding personnel decision making (raises, promotions, team configuration) or personnel development (training, assignments, and mentoring), depending on how they are used.[1] Yet the foundations of good systems are common to all.

Like the traditional review, social recognition works best when several foundational conditions are understood. (You'll find more operational detail in the Appendix of this book.)

Social Architecture Supports Culture

Social architecture is to culture what a foundation, beams, and joists are to a building. Social architecture includes communication, traditions, authority, privileges, behaviors, and relationships. It is the result of formal structures like an organization chart, informal (unwritten) habits like "how we communicate" or "how we do meetings," and aspects of relationships like trust, respect, and fear. It includes behavior cues like how people dress and how they talk to one another. It includes how excellence is recognized and rewarded, because that's a way of talking about the implementation of culture.

A company's social architecture is mostly informal but nonetheless powerful, because people are social beings, able to pick up cultural cues quickly and then consciously conform to them, defy them, or adapt them to their personal style.

Social architecture translates particular values into particular behaviors. For example, it takes a value like "determination" and translates it into situational behaviors like, "No matter what, we will never give up on a sale." It is the framework of communication, positive and negative reinforcement, public and private knowledge, and cultural cues that determine how the company will operate. It includes the hierarchy of authority and reward, the transparency of information, and even the manners and traditions of the company.

Social architecture exists because no manager can be everywhere, on every phone call, standing beside every employee whenever they're doing something. It's the set of behavioral norms that define a culture—"what you do when nobody is looking."

The Social Graph

Social architecture makes it possible to construct a *social graph* of a person's behavior and performance if enough people—the crowd surrounding a person's work—evaluate his or her behavior against a company's goals and values. Over time, a graph of how values are acted upon (or ignored) is built by many small evaluations, using social recognition.

When recognition of a person's good work is matched to the values of the company, a social graph of individual performance can be made. Figure 6.1 is a simple illustration of the idea, with four company values shown. (We revisit this figure in Chapter 7.).

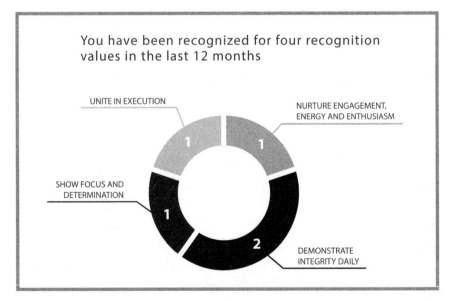

Figure 6.1 A values-based social graph

Now individual acts are not only recognized, but the data can monitor how actions are related to overall values. As Lori Gaytan of IHG comments, social recognition thus makes it possible to visualize the connections among actions, values, and results. She says, "We can directly correlate culture and people to our business results. . . . For the first time, we're able to measure the adoption of culture throughout the organization and know which employees are living our values."[2]

Any initiative in performance management can go awry if best practices are left behind. Our studies with customers and research partners, as well as long-term experience, have identified several practices that make social recognition most effective in improving performance.

Social recognition can create a Positivity Dominated Workplace provided it is executed with broad participation. It must unite employees around shared values. It must be championed by management and reinforced through ongoing communications. It must offer recognition and rewards that are weighted to the significance of the behavior observed. Let's look at these must-haves in detail:

Broad Participation

Just like traditional performance reviews, broad participation is essential for success. A successful social recognition program is characterized by a high degree of interactions, that is, with 80+ percent of the workforce participating annually, and 1–2 percent of payroll used for recognizing achievement in the form of small, incremental awards.

Best practices (as documented in a Stanford Graduate School of Business case study) are that if the recognition program is promoted so that at least 5 percent of the workforce receives a recognition award each week, a critical mass will be achieved and the program will maintain and promote itself. The program reaches that tipping point where most employees know the program and embrace its goals.[3] In practice, some employees will receive two awards in a year, and some will receive six.

The 2008 Stanford case study focused on the social recognition program at Intuit, called "Spotlight." Intuit's 8,200 global employees awarded 20,000 recognition moments in the first year and 26,000 the following year. Eighty-five percent of Intuit's employees received awards each year, and employee opinion surveys showed that employees felt that their accomplishments were recognized by the company.

The Intuit case study found that when you get to 5–8 percent weekly cadence (that is, 5–8 percent of the workforce being recognized per week), you have higher penetration, higher engagement, and a self-sustaining program (see Figure 6.2).

"Saying thank you in a meaningful way is a powerful lever as part of an organization's overall performance feedback mechanisms," said Jim Grenier, the former vice president of human resources at Intuit who directed the case study with Stanford Business School professor Hayagreeva Rao. Grenier pointed out the importance of broad implementation: "Having the right tools that are easy for employees to use can increase adoption. Most importantly, however, is how the different pieces

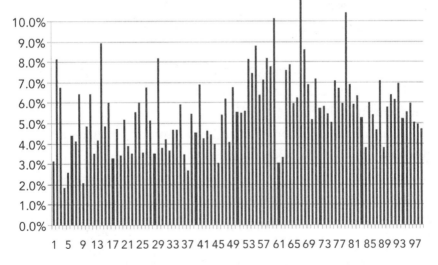

RECOGNITION PROGRAM ADOPTION

WEEKLY AWARDS AT INTUIT, AS A PERCENT OF EMPLOYEES, FROM LAUNCH OF SPOTLIGHT.

Figure 6.2 Weekly awards at Intuit

of a program are all connected to drive the right messages to teams and individuals, thus building momentum for success and growth."[4]

Intuit's Spotlight program continues to be a key way HR reinforces its culture. It wants employees to feel valued. In fact, recent employee surveys conducted by the company show that 90 percent of employees are proud to work for the company.

Shared Values

Management teams of most companies have spent countless hours concisely defining their company's values and honing their company's mission that inspire employees to achieve strategic goals. For a company's values to have an impact on employee behavior and performance, they must be understood in the same way by all employees regardless of position, division, or geographic location.

Figure 6.3 illustrates how JetBlue broadcasts its values in the company headquarters.

Figure 6.3 Visible values in JetBlue headquarters

Figure 6.4 shows IHG values, which are called Winning Ways.

Of course, it's not just about putting words on a wall. JetBlue and IHG strive for a culture in which the values they display on the wall are lived every day by every employee.

Do the right thing   Show we care   Aim higher

Celebrate difference   Work better together

Figure 6.4 IHG values, Winning Ways

To achieve this level of common understanding, managers must clearly and consistently communicate the organization's values. This task can be diluted not only by a company's scale but also by a varied and diverse workforce (especially in global companies). Furthermore, the task of communicating is complicated by variability in communication skills among managers as well as individual managers' perceptions of the relative worth of certain values. To manage is to choose among multiple options, and business situations inevitably cause a manager to choose in the moment between, for example, customer satisfaction and greater efficiency. Deeply ingrained values point the way to resolve these conflicting options.

Shared values are taught, retaught, and honored when social recognition draws attention to specific behaviors referencing a specific company value. Of course, the individual being recognized is reminded of the values demonstrated. If the recognition is public, or requires approval, the behaviors and values are doubly reinforced. If all recognition within a set time is shared in a team meeting, then entire teams will be reminded of the company's values. In large, globally distributed companies this is virtually the only way to make the company values come off the wall and come alive for every employee.

Tom Aurelio, vice president of global human resources at Symantec, explained the importance of emphasizing shared values in a social recognition program at this global leader in information security and storage.

By 2008, following a series of acquisitions, Symantec grew from 6,500 employees to 14,000 in a very short period of time, leaving the company with a "culture of many different cultures." To evolve toward one unified culture, leadership needed to educate everyone about a single set of company values, create open lines of communications with employees, and foster a program to build trust among all employees everywhere in the world.

Tom noted that the emphasis on shared values allowed him to focus on critical gaps. "We are a values based organization, and we're in the technology space. A culture of innovation is pretty much ingrained in what we do. One of the great advantages of [social recognition] is that we can really monitor how much of our rewards are going towards innovation. If we realize that we are starting to slip a little bit, we can do the right programs or plug the right projects in place that will drive innovation."[5]

Communication

Anyone who has managed a performance process knows that communication is one of the great challenges. There's a latent unease between manager and employee when it comes to judging performance, not only from the employee who is being judged but also from the manager who wants to keep the lines of communication open but fears the risk of alienating staff members.

Open, honest, and frequent communication among employees goes a long way toward making the process appear legitimate to all. Social recognition of performance helps communication by relying on trusted peer-to-peer input and by repeated small notations of accomplishment.

Recognition should happen somewhere in the company every day. That means it's got to be promoted, explained, advertised, and marketed to *and by* every employee. Fortunately, the nature of a recognition program makes it a natural fit for today's viral communications methods.

Creating a Positivity Dominated Workplace is an open-ended, continuous practice. Performance appraisals tend to be annualized events, and employees have an acute, short-term incentive to pay attention and engage. Watching for moments to recognize good performance in real time should be a workplace habit.

A social program with a high penetration rate actually markets itself through the approval process. For example, I'm nominating you for an award. I get approval from my manager. When I give the award, my manager and the department manager are copied on the notice. Now four people are aware of the award. If 5 percent of the workforce receives an award every week, up to 15 or 20 percent of the workforce—and a high number of managers—are reminded of the recognition program every week. Awareness becomes self-perpetuating.

Moving the entire company from no awareness of social recognition to high awareness requires a strong launch of the program with a clear understanding of its meaning for performance management. As awareness becomes self-perpetuating, the formal message of a Positivity

A Self-Regulating Recognition Budget

Maybe a long line of approvals for performance rewards are overrated. What if managers were simply given a recognition budget and guidelines on award levels, and they didn't need approvals? As long as the awards are tracked and analyzed, the controls are in place to have an effective recognition program. The program becomes self-regulating. The program can also be designed to "throttle back" as aggregate awards approach the budget limit. A side benefit of this practice: Managers gain more autonomy and accountability for their main job, which is managing people!

Dominated Workplace shifts to celebrating the awards themselves. Even as valuable recognition data go into the system, the positivity of the program improves morale and employees' sense of progress.

Weighted Awards

Making the monetary value of recognition awards proportional to the achievement or behavior is a key indicator of the importance of the act being recognized. The award might simply be public appreciation, such as the one shown at the end of Chapter 4. That's appropriate for a peer-inspired "high five" for a small act or a great attitude. For larger accomplishments, awards with various monetary values indicate the magnitude of the accomplishment to all.

People crave affirmation that their actions are important and meaningful, but understand that actions have different effects on the bottom line. Employees should have a simple concept of how different award levels are set, as is shown in Table 6.1.

Award level (examples)	Level of effort	Scope of impact
A = $50 value	Extra contribution	Personal performance impact
B = $150 value	Unusually strong contribution or unusually tough challenge met	Department-wide impact
C = $500 value	Extraordinary contribution or extraordinary challenge met	Companywide impact

Table 6.1 Award weighting strategies scale according to contribution. Later, this data will help categorize effort.

Without weighted awards, employees can quickly become cynical about the program. After all, you wouldn't recognize and reward someone who was instrumental in developing a new innovation that led to millions in new product revenue the same way you would reward someone who contributed to a team's success in resolving a sticky client situation. Both contributions deserve recognition and validation but not at the same level.

Bringing Social Recognition into the Workplace

A social recognition program must have executive support. The very presence of social recognition means that top leadership is sending the message, "We trust our people to help judge performance themselves." This is a dramatic change from the top-down mindset that describes most performance review systems. Executives need to throw their moral and strategic weight behind social recognition to ensure its importance.

In my experience, a social recognition performance component needs to have the public support of a very senior executive—the CEO if possible, followed by the head of HR. This "trust initiative" needs a champion at the top in more than one communication. For greatest program impact, one or more executive sponsors must publicly agree to monitor and discuss the implementation of the program and, as it succeeds, to champion its results.

If executives do this, employees will know that social recognition is as important as the annual performance review because it will be inextricably *part* of that review.

Executives should also publicly and loudly participate in the program themselves. This might be hard for those who see themselves at such a level of accomplishment and self-motivation that they do not need internal recognition, but strong leaders know that their participation in company initiatives validates the program more than any other action. The example of executives recognizing employees for performance, from the most experienced executive vice president to the newest receptionist, demonstrates that crowdsourcing performance reviews is valid, powerful, and expected of everyone.

The Heroic Leader Meets Dunbar's Number

Worldwide, organizations celebrate the heroic leader—the man or woman whose vision and will create (and presumably enforce) a particular culture. Business media have glorified leaders such as Lee Iacocca of Chrysler, Bill Gates of Microsoft, Steve Jobs of Apple, Lou Gerstner

Moving from Top-Down to Bottom-Up

According to research firm Gartner, social recognition programs can help improve performance while decreasing reliance solely on manager and executive feedback. In the report, Gartner managing vice president Jim Holincheck wrote, "Leading organizations will start to move toward more bottom-up feedback, recognition and rewards." Managers can see the level of frequency of recognition and performance feedback for individual employees. As a result, "Senior executives can use this data to see if manager performance decisions align with what coworkers indicate through their actions."[6]

of IBM, and Herb Kelleher of Southwest Airlines. Each built a social architecture to support a cultural vision, and this was a key development because each of these leaders left a lasting company after their time at the helm ended.

Today's business leaders, from Amazon's Jeff Bezos to Facebook's Mark Zuckerberg and Google's Larry Page, are celebrated for their cultural vision as well as their technical acumen. Today's leaders stress a culture of accountability, openness, speed, and teamwork that reflects the interdependent nature of their work, and they are relentlessly focused on performance management, from their notoriously demanding job interviews to performance reviews.

Jack Welch led GE through enormous changes—the Work-Out program for breaking down bureaucracy and hierarchy and Six-Sigma processes are just two he oversaw—and his vision, uncompromising standards, and astute use of media aided his success. GE was and is a vast, worldwide organization with hundreds of thousands of employees in scores of countries. He couldn't meet with every employee to persuade each one to perform to his standards in his way. He needed a methodology and a structure that would nurture the values he deemed most important. So he posited a set of principles that defined how work would be measured, evaluated, and judged. Leveraging the existing social architecture, Welch improved communication and impressed every employee with his determination to fight for his values.

Social architecture doesn't require a public figure like Welch for it to be enormously effective. Some of the most successful companies in the world have had a succession of "quiet" CEOs. Johnson & Johnson, for example, expresses its values in "Our Credo," a statement that describes its responsibilities to doctors, nurses, patients, families, employees, communities, and, finally, shareholders. Outlined are specific behavioral guidelines ("Compensation must be fair and adequate, and working conditions clean, orderly, and safe") that are flexible enough to apply across countries, businesses, and cultures.

When a large environment is aligned along just a few values, there is little ambiguity. A hundred signals a day promote their adoption. (Any manager or line worker can determine whether a workplace is "clean, orderly, and safe.") And a hundred times a day, people at Johnson & Johnson can recognize the right values in action.

At the other end of the size spectrum, the start-up organization also benefits from a deliberate social architecture. Start-ups classically begin with a few people, a vision, and an obsessive focus on just one or two central ideas. That focus is critical when a company is small and the CEO

Executive Insight

"The middle 70 percent are managed differently. This group of people is enormously valuable to any company; you simply cannot function without their skills, energy, and commitment. After all, they are the majority of your employees. But everyone in the middle 70 needs to be motivated, and made to feel as if they truly belong. You do not want to lose the vast majority of your middle 70—you want to improve them."

—Jack Welch, *Winning*[7]

can promote an idea face to face with 10 or 50 or 100 employees. But daily interaction with employees for a start-up executive becomes impossible as the company grows. It's the nature of scaling a company. There will be people the CEO won't see on a daily basis, so the cult of personality wanes.

There's a limit to the number of close relationships a human can maintain. Oxford Professor Robin Dunbar's studies of social networks (from holiday card lists to the world's surviving hunter-gatherer tribes) reveal that they max out at about 150 members. Dunbar has said that it's a simple cognitive limit—150 meaningful relationships is the largest social network most people can maintain. Beyond that, relationships tend to diminish in significance and strength.

A leader can inspire others through words, but "Dunbar's number" means that the cohesive "tribe" of close relationships remains at about 150 per person. This means that even a heroic, iconic leader must extend relationships through values, ideas, stories, and the networks of people who pass them along. This is crowdsourced culture management—delegating responsibility to transmit the culture. The true heroic leader builds an organization that translates his or her beliefs into a culture.

Zappos.com is a popular example of successfully translating the values of a hero CEO deep within an organization as it experiences explosive growth. A key value for Zappos.com is its nonnegotiable, obsessive, 24/7 devotion to customer service. The company's CEO, Tony Hsieh, built the company around it. (Motto: "At Zappos.com, customer service is everything. In fact, it's the entire company.") Early on, Tony and his executive team could promote these values by power of example, by asking, "How will this affect the customer?" at every opportunity, and by rewarding and recognizing workers who shared the company's obsession with customer satisfaction. As the company grew, Tony and his team could hire like-minded managers who demonstrated their passion for customer satisfaction in their actions. Today the company has sales of more than $1 billion, and each new employee is hired on the basis of his or her values—putting the customer first—and publicly or privately honored for any demonstration of that value. When Jeff Bezos,

Amazon.com's CEO, announced the purchase of Zappos.com in July 2009, he credited the company's obsession with customer service for his decision. Bezos said that such a company made him "weak in the knees"—to the tune of around $900 million—and added that he wasn't going to change a thing.

For every Tony Hsieh there are a thousand CEOs less charismatic, and for them it is imperative that every employee knows and propagates the cultural values of the company. Crowdsourcing helps you jump over Dunbar's number.

Implementing Social Recognition

Implementing social recognition in a workplace that has used only traditional methods of performance management is best done in four steps:

1. Decide how traditional reviews and social recognition will work together.
2. Budget for the social recognition program.
3. Phase in a social recognition system.
4. Measure and adjust the budget as needed.

Decide How Traditional Reviews and Social Recognition Will Work Together

Every 6 or 12 months, a manager meets one-on-one with an employee in a familiar ritual: they review written goals, compare them to accomplishments in the preceding months, talk about behaviors to "continue, stop, or change," and wrap up with a discussion about the next period's goals. If both are skilled at the review process, they have brought concrete examples of accomplishments and problem areas. Perhaps the employee will seek coaching on a career path or in an area of growth.

In between these formal reviews, managers are expected to monitor performance against expectations. Where performance is good, they give recognition and encouragement. Where performance is lacking, they offer coaching or don't give recognition. These check-ins might be informal or rigorous. Depending on the temperaments involved, managers might keep a close watch on how a staffer is doing, or they might be more hands off.

Social recognition enhances both these review methods. In the short term, a manager can recognize and reward behavior directly, granting a monetary-value award and broadcasting congratulations for a job exceptionally well done. Indirectly, other employees notice great work, and their accolades are captured in the manager's records. In both cases, social recognition provides concrete stories of accomplishment, which over time become part of the performance conversation between manager and employee.

Specific, time-bound stories are more effective in performance management than abstractions. Human beings are hardwired to remember stories, and telling a story creates connections among all the factors that go into work: relationships, deadlines, resources, actions taken, and alternative actions.

In the long term, social recognition nominations feed the traditional review by relating stories of accomplishment to written goals. Stories illuminate the path taken to goals that are hardwired and objective (sales quotas) or abstract and subjective ("delight customers").

Managers approve awards through the social recognition database and applications; this keeps them on top of activity in their groups. Thus managers have a tool to monitor the recognition program and the positive work behaviors occurring both in front of them and out of their sight. All participants learn more about the work community's tasks, inspirations, ideas, values, and behaviors. As with social networking software, all share a free-flowing workplace narrative.

Because recognition events happen spontaneously, social recognition is a real-time management tool; managers pick up information as employees are nominated for awards and the awards are approved. In the first year, the number of these stories typically grows slowly, but the growth accelerates as more employees at every level participate. Soon recognition data can be more formally linked to performance assessment.

"Our pay raises and bonuses are based on objective criteria."

If pay were always based on objective criteria, we could call performance reviews at least fair in theory. But show me a truly objective reviewer! Managers are human, subject to errors of omission, unconscious bias, poor self-management, and yes, poor performance in their roles as performance managers.

MYTH**BUSTER**

Budget Strategically

Budgeting for a social recognition program is absolutely critical. You need to get 80+ percent penetration of a recognition program in the workforce for the aggregate data to be statistically reliable and accurate. (You really want 80 percent, because then the data really take off.) Because high penetration is a must, we have found the budget success point to be at least 1 percent of the payroll for awards. As noted earlier, HR consultancy WorldatWork found in 2011 that organizations are budgeting an average of 2 percent of the payroll budget to be used for recognition programs; however, the median amount budgeted in 2011 is 1 percent.[8] Some of my clients have found the program to be so successful that they raise the budget after starting at the average.

One simple beginning structure is to allocate 10 percent of existing bonus money to a social recognition program.[9] Let's say that Mary's annual bonus is set at $5,000. Her manager sets MBO goals for $4,500, and the remaining $500 is allocated to a social recognition pool. Potentially, Mary could receive up to $500 in a number of small awards for which she was nominated by her peers, internal customers, or manager, and the recognition database tracks her awards. A common difference is that social recognition awards reinforce positive behavior more effectively than do long-term bonuses because they are immediate and tied to specific behaviors. We often find that these cumulative recognition moments, where Mary receives on-the-spot bonuses equivalent to $50 or $100, do a better job of moving the needle on her performance and her alignment with the culture of the company.

After starting at a 10/90 percent mix, you might find that social recognition awards given through the year by peers move the needle on performance more effectively than a year-end bonus, and so you change the allocation to 20/80 percent or 30/70 percent in the bonus pool. Depending on the company's size and culture, the best formula might be different. Research firm Gartner recommends that HR leaders study the business results of all bonus awards as the program progresses over several years.[10] Over time the right mix of formal bonus and social recognition budget allocation will be clear from the data.

For those employees who don't currently participate in any bonus plan, social recognition is a huge step forward. With a program in place, even the lowest-paying or most routine-bound job position has the capacity for rewards and the social incentive to excel. The potential and proven benefits of social recognition, and its symbiosis with the traditional performance review, make a compelling case that money should be allocated for all employees.

Incidentally, large companies are already spending 1 percent or more of payroll in ad hoc recognition programs; they just don't know it. Those well-intentioned, informal acts of recognition—taking the department out for dinner or buying tickets to the ball game as a thank you—tend to be obscured as expenses in travel and entertainment budgets. Indirect costs like tax liabilities, duplication of effort, and corporate governance rules add to the expense of ad hoc programs. We've known CFOs who have tried to separate these expenses to achieve a real view of what informal recognition costs, and they never get to the bottom of it.

Phase In a Program

As the budget strategy implies, phasing in a social recognition program is a matter of adding it to established routines (as opposed to throwing out routine and starting from scratch). Gartner recommends running a test of the social recognition program alongside existing pay-for-performance programs.

There are good reasons to test a program across the entire employee population, rather than with a small test group. As a culture management tool, social recognition encourages alignment with company values regardless of an employee's position, prestige, or location. Since different subcultures exist among groups in a company (think "competitive" sales vs. "cooperative" design, or "hard skills" finance vs. "soft skills" marketing), recognition will be integrated into those cultures somewhat differently. Comparing the resulting data among groups yields rich insights. One group might adopt the new system quickly with its members becoming ambassadors to other groups.

Rolling out a recognition program does require training and communication; this is most efficiently shared with everyone. In the days of digital marketing, it is cheaper and more efficient to have one launch for everyone rather than many launches or separate ones for each group.

Lastly, since a social recognition program offers tangible rewards, everyone should have a chance to get in the game as soon as possible.

A robust social recognition system of any size should produce measurable results. Relevant metrics should gauge how the system is being implemented (participation) and its effect on specific workplace goals (success).

Measure and Adjust the Budget as Needed

Participation is fundamental to success. One difficulty we've witnessed in some recognition systems is a struggle to achieve adoption by a supermajority of employees. Unless 80+ percent of employees and managers are participating, the system will render an incomplete picture of the social graph—and when you have an incomplete picture of the social graph, you don't really have the social graph. Comparison between groups becomes difficult, and data become questionable: Even 100 percent reliable data won't yield cultural insights if it's measuring only 20 percent of the population.

Problems in social recognition systems might include complexity, in which the system is just too hard to use (remember the power of a social system is its voluntary nature; it's best not to discourage that); lack of relevant rewards; poor communication of its benefits; or even residual cynicism and inertia (this is a threat in companies that suffer from the shortcomings of the traditional performance review, such as a lack of trust). The potential problems have to be thought through in advance with that 80 percent participation goal in mind.

The simplest case for high participation is identical to the case for having every manager conduct a traditional performance review: If you have a tool that is even moderately able to improve performance, you should deploy it across the board.

As the social recognition program gets under way and gains momentum, success metrics should be applied to monitor its effectiveness. Metrics must certainly be tailored to corporate goals; in our experience, the most powerful combine traditional performance goals and cultural cues. For example:

- Employees hitting or exceeding performance goals of all kinds (income, efficiency, Six-Sigma, innovation, customer satisfaction, and the like)
- An increasing employee net promoter score (via surveys)[11]
- Better employee retention rates
- Increased scores in traditional reviews (from managers)
- Increased scores in internal surveys of company values (employee trust, ease of doing business; e.g., "I'm given the tools I need to do my job.")
- Increased scores in employee engagement surveys
- Increased scores in employee recognition and appreciation metrics on employment surveys
- Increased customer service/satisfaction scores

As participation increases, the data set grows more detailed, and management can look deeper into the performance social graph of the organization. Who is truly engaged? Which departments seem to be self-propelled, and which are lagging? Where are employees most satisfied, most alert to new opportunities, or living the company values most thoroughly? All this appears in a social graph, identifying places where management can accelerate performance and find the next generation of leaders.

Over time, HR should return to budgets, balancing the proportions of payroll, benefit, and incentive money to gain maximum performance from the performance systems themselves.

As the employee "crowd" works increasingly with management to improve performance, social recognition inspires continuous improvement and goes beyond performance management to create a self-perpetuating culture.

Don't Discard the Traditional Review Entirely

I say earlier that adding social recognition to the traditional review is preferable to switching to a 100 percent crowdsourced model. This is because businesses are subject to legal requirements in their interactions with employees, and performance systems leave an audit trail. Traditional performance systems do some things that crowdsourcing alone can't do as well, such as quantifying revenue delivery compared to companywide financial goals.

There are also process benefits from preserving current performance review systems. Some managers simply need the structure of a defined A–Z process. Human resources systems are set up around established performance systems and use them to monitor progress from one year to another. Furthermore, employees who transition to other companies deserve some common language about their performance to take with them so they can still say, for example, "I exceed expectations in four out of five categories every year."

The crowdsourced review in practice preserves the best of traditional performance management. Social recognition fixes the traditional review's shortcomings.

Years of Service Awards

There's a lot of negativity about programs that just reward tenure in the form of anniversary awards. Today's business culture recognizes achievement and understands that long tenure is a vanishing attribute; the old "gold watch" award seems like a relic of the past.

In my company, we had a "eureka moment" when we reintroduced a years-of-service award on a modern social platform that allowed people to add congratulations to the award. The experience of seeing people being rewarded for certain amounts of tenure, and the different celebration moments that inspired the crowd, was extraordinary. Certain individuals who had worked with us for a long time had no idea how far their impact went. Their years-of-service milestone, in a social setting, set off a wildfire of goodwill with dozens of people piling on congratulations, recalling stories from the company's history, and joining in a spirit of celebration. This outpouring of goodwill was positive for everyone and for the company culture.

A modern years-of-service program gives people the ability to celebrate an employee's tangible and intangible contributions. When it's tied into a social recognition program, it allows the crowd to celebrate the contributions of truly great employees and provides a natural time to do that. Social recognition tends to focus on performance in the here and now, with many awards given at the micro level.

A milestone like a certain number of years of service inspires the crowd (most of whom have typically not been at the company for a long time) to join the manager in taking a step back and celebrating the full impact of an employee's long-term contribution. As the crowd reflects on the cumulative achievements of a long-term employee, individuals consider the progress of the company itself.

Business journalism often reviews the arc of an executive's career because years of achievement put today's work in context. Years-of-service events do the same internally. They honor the arc of progress in a person's work. They confer dignity and add to the narrative of the company as a whole. Unlike a transactional program, using social recognition to rejuvenate years of service awards magnifies and broadcasts an employee's historical achievements.

Incorporating social recognition elements into years-of-service milestones can also help new managers. They are given a treasure trove of past insights/anecdotes to show them how valued their employee is. It also sets them up to properly give years-of-service awards in the future—since they now have knowledge of the employee's performance and work since before the manager joined the company.

In my experience, years-of-service awards are among the most popular with the crowd participating in the award because these awards are focused on the whole person, which humanizes a workplace and strengthens the social ties among all.

7 | Putting the Crowdsourced Performance Review into Practice

Liz and Dana discussed Dana's traditional performance review quickly. Like her previous reviews, the checklist indicated that Dana was an outstanding project manager. Once again, the form registered a row of 4s and 5s. After finishing the form, Liz asked Dana to join her at her computer. She opened Dana's social recognition dashboard report, and they began to review the charts and graphs Dana's peers had created over the year.

"This is the first time your review won't be just a bunch of numbers and comments," said Liz. "No more check, check, check, Dana's excellent, blah blah."

Dana laughed a little nervously, and said, "Well, checklists are a project manager's life, right?"

"But now we have more than a checklist," Liz continued, studying the social recognition dashboard on her screen. "Let's go back to the GTY prototyping project and see what your colleagues *here and overseas said about your work. You received several awards for making things work so smoothly. What do you think made it special?"*

Dana said, "GTY was the first global prototyping initiative, and the challenge was coordinating our project execution with the design and development teams in England and Germany."

Liz and Dana revisited four different recognition awards, each given for a different project. The discussion ranged from tactical learning to Hydrolab values. Liz could see that Dana had given thought to each of the values. She was confident that she'd made the right choices in rating Dana's performance, and she looked forward to the surprise opportunity she would offer Dana at the end of the review.

Bestselling business writer Dan Pink offers this cringe-worthy vision of the traditional performance review: "Performance reviews are rarely authentic conversations. More often, they are the West's form of kabuki theater—highly stylized rituals in which people recite predictable lines in a formulaic way and hope the experience ends very quickly.[1]

What if the performance review were an authentic conversation? Social media have moved companies to humanize their communications with customers, prospects, and vendors. Expectations have changed within the company as well. People want and deserve a genuine, unguarded conversation about performance. That's what we're striving to produce with the addition of social recognition, and the key to this in practice is to use the narrative power of social recognition to make the performance review authentic.

A business conversation, not a friendly chat, is the right objective. Both sides approach the review cautiously because the typical version has been set up as a kind of negotiation. The employee wants to sell himself as high achieving, and worthy of "praise and a raise." He might see even constructive criticism as a threat to his prospects and maybe his job. The manager wants to give her fairest assessment of the employee's performance, offer some suggestions, and allocate a limited salary budget most productively among all staffers. She likely wants to avoid conflict, and even if she's comfortable with tough discussions, she wants to avoid having to confront employee defensiveness. Looming over all this at many companies is the perennial question of "separating" the performance discussion from the merit pay discussion, as if they could be truly separate.

Ideally, the performance review should be a business discussion with both parties working toward the same goal, that is, analyzing performance based on facts, finding ways to improve performance at whatever level, and allocating money fairly. The dynamic tension of the traditional review, however, makes it almost impossible for both individuals to detach emotionally from the conversation and the outcome. Thus the kabuki theater, and the lost opportunity to leverage performance management to actually improve performance.

We can do better. In the following pages, I sketch out a vision of how social recognition and the traditional review combine to make that business conversation narrative come alive. At last, the employee and the manager will be working side by side, instead of in anxious negotiation.

For this chapter's suggestions, I address you, the manager, directly. You'll learn a step-by-step process for integrating the crowdsourced performance data of social recognition with your traditional review format as you:

- Prepare for the review (both employee and manager).
- Combine the best of the traditional review with social recognition to manage a complete review as well as an authentic conversation.
- Relate recognition received by an employee to create a narrative of performance.
- Plan the future development and advancement of the employee.
- Weigh the pros and cons of negative feedback.

The Generic Performance Review

For the sake of clarity, I use the classic "general factors" review in this chapter as a model. It's familiar to any manager as the form that lists job duties and ranks the employee's performance along a scale. It looks like the sample from *Entrepreneur* magazine in Figure 7.1.

The *Entrepreneur* sample has a four-part scale ranging from "outstanding" to "improvement needed." Others rate performance on a scale of 1–5, or use the familiar scale of "exceeds expectations," "meets expectations," and "does not meet expectations."[2]

Sometimes a performance instrument rates specific deliverables in a job such as product release times or average time to resolve a customer issue. There are scores of variations on these models but the concept generally is set in the following sequence:

1. State the work factor, behavior, goal, or expectation.
2. Rate the quality of the employee's work.
3. Comment.

The "comment" is all the room the manager has to put some nuance on a performance metric, to justify his or her decision, and to give details about any employee's performance in the range from stupendous to mediocre. Social recognition informs the manager's judgment of an employee's work and supplies the narrative that will make the comment area meaningful in terms of actually detailing performance. (See Figure 7.1.)

I suggest starting with an orientation toward social recognition moments by grounding the discussion at the outset in specific behaviors. Review in general terms what social recognition says about the employee's performance (see the examples later in this chapter) and then proceed to the traditional instrument, using examples from social recognition to create a meaningful dialogue about the employee's work year.

Why is this a good idea? It links specific behavior to the appraisal. Instead of the manager offering a vague or subjective impression of the quality of work, it focuses on actual work done, real projects, and remem-

Employee Name:_____ Job Title: _____

Date of Hire:_____ Department: _____ Supervisor:_____

Annual Review ☐   90 day Review ☐   Review Period: From _____ To _____

Purpose: The purpose of conducting the Performance Appraisal is to: Develop better communication between the employee and the supervisor; Improve the quality of work; Increase productivity; and Promote employee development. **Performance Rating Categories:** Consider the employee's performance in each category and designate the level of performance that most accurately describes his/her job performance.

O – Outstanding. Employee consistently exceeds position expectations with virtually no detected preventable/controllable errors, requiring little or no supervision.

M – Meets Expectation. Competent & dependable performance level. Meets the performance standards and objectives of the job without constant follow-up / direction.

E – Exceeds Expectation. Results clearly **exceed** position requirements on a regular basis. Performance is of high quality and is achieved on a consistent basis.

I – Improvement Needed. Employee does not meet performance objectives on a regular basis and has difficulty following through with tasks. Requires constant follow-up and / or supervision.

N/A – Not applicable or too soon to rate.

I.   GENERAL FACTORS

1. **Quality –** The extent to which an employee's work is completed thoroughly and correctly following established process & procedures. Required paperwork is thorough and neat.

    ☐ **Outstanding**   ☐ **Exceeds Expectations**   ☐ **Meets Expectations**   ☐ **Improvement Needed**

    Specific Examples / Comments: _____

    _____

    _____

2. **Productivity / Independence / Reliability -** The extent to which an employee produces a significant volume of work efficiently in a specified period of time. Ability to work independently with little or no direction/ follow-up to complete tasks / job assignment.

    ☐ **Outstanding**   ☐ **Exceeds Expectations**   ☐ **Meets Expectations**   ☐ **Improvement Needed**

    Specific Examples / Comments: _____

    _____

    _____

3. **Job Knowledge -** The extent to which an employee possesses and demonstrates an understating of the work instructions, processes, equipment and materials required to perform the job. Employee possesses the practical and technical knowledge required of the job.

    ☐ **Outstanding**   ☐ **Exceeds Expectations**   ☐ **Meets Expectations**   ☐ **Improvement Needed**

    Specific Examples / Comments: _____

    _____

    _____

4. **Interpersonal Relationships / Cooperation / Commitment –** The extent to which employee is willing and demonstrates the ability to cooperate, work and communicate with coworkers, supervisors, subordinates and/or outside contacts.   Employee accepts and responds to change in a positive manner. Accepts job assignments and additional duties willingly, takes responsibility for own performance and job assignments.

    ☐ **Outstanding**   ☐ **Exceeds Expectations**   ☐ **Meets Expectations**   ☐ **Improvement Needed**

    Specific Examples / Comments: _____

    _____

    _____

Figure 7.1 Sample "general factors" review form

bered moments. Abstraction is swept away, and a real conversation can be held about real events. From the employee's point of view, the conversation is really about performance, not about whether the manager is interpreting quality of work accurately. Therefore starting this way establishes trust at the outset.

This combined method, beginning with social recognition, also gets the discussion off to a positive start as a business conversation, which is the opposite of the tortured kabuki theater that Dan Pink described.

The traditional focus points of a performance review are competencies (what the employee can do), skills (how the employee works), and goals (what the work must accomplish). There is often no formal connection to company values. Social recognition provides concrete instances, noted in real behaviors by the crowd, of both competencies and skills, and it documents the achieved goals. It then goes further to relate all these behaviors and outcomes to values.

Prepare for the Review

It's a business truism that there should be no surprises in a performance review. If a manager has provided regular feedback and coaching throughout the year, the employee already knows how he or she is doing. An annual performance assessment should confirm this impression, discuss the present situation, and plan for the future.

Social recognition provides feedback from the crowd to the individual and his or her manager throughout the year. Preparing for the annual performance review, then, amounts to looking back at the information that has already been shared. It really is a review—no surprises. What is new with social recognition is the depth and detail of information available.

The work of the formal review begins well before its scheduled date. First, the manager should explain the performance review process, working with HR when appropriate. Typically, the process is explained in an e-mail to everyone, and managers meet with members of their staff to make sure that the process is clear. This is the time to remind employees that social recognition input will be used in the review process. Point out that crowdsourcing input on performance management is a key benefit of the social recognition system and that it benefits the managers by providing input about performance from the people who have been best able to witness it. (Communicating this is initially part of setting up a social recognition program; now it's a reminder that social recognition is a serious management tool and empowers every employee to contribute to the performance of the organization.)

Presenting the crowdsourced performance review, HR should communicate to all that it is the manager's responsibility to assess and improve the performance of his or her staff, and social recognition is a vital input to this process, making it richer and more broad-based than relying on one set of eyes alone. HR might also stress that the social recognition information is helpful to managers in their role as coach and mentor and that it is helpful to all when talking about employee strengths, needs, and ambitions.

How Employees Prepare

Two weeks before the review, managers should invite employees to engage in the process by preparing a self-assessment according to the traditional method you've been using and also using the social recognition moments they have received to analyze their performance. One of the easiest ways for an employee to prepare is to create stories about their recognition moments in the familiar job-interview technique called SAR (situation, action, result). Recognition makes the employee's task easier because he or she has a record of actions that earned recognition, just as the manager does.

Thus an employee responsible for setting up an annual sales meeting and who received recognition for resolving an unexpected last-minute change might prepare the following notes:

- *Situation.* The sales vice president's presentation was final ten days before the sales meeting, and all the staging of her speech was set. However, one week before the meeting, a vice president of HR of a local client company who was to speak at the sales meeting had a family crisis and could not attend. The client said he would provide a substitute, but that person was not as familiar with our product or the story. The substitute was willing but nervous about representing his company.

- *Action.* I spent two days at the client company's HQ with the substitute guest, previewing the sales meeting, demonstrating our product, and coaching him with touches like a color "cheat sheet" of our executive team and key sales representatives. I wrote a short speech for our sales director to introduce the new person and got an official portrait and bio information for our design staff to change in the PowerPoint presentation. On the morning of the sales conference, I rehearsed the substitute. I acted as his "personal concierge" for the meeting.
- *Result.* The substitute did a great job of firing up our sales team along with our VP, and established relationships with our sales and executive teams. Six months later, he is our principal contact with the client. I received recognition from our VP of sales and the event marketing team in our stated values of "show focus and determination" and "demonstrate integrity daily."

This preparation moves the employee away from the mindset in which she's worrying about whether her self-appraisal "rating" is justified and more into an analysis of why she was recognized for outstanding performance. It ties her actions directly to company values (which is part of the recognition model). Based on the positive reaction of the crowd around her—the genesis of this is a recognition moment—she is ready to discuss the details of her performance with confidence.

If an employee completes this process for all of her principle goals, roles, and/or responsibilities, she will go into the review with a much richer set of impressions than she might have by simply checking off a box marked "satisfactory."

For those goals or responsibilities for which no recognition award has been given, the employee can still prepare examples, and the discussion can include both those examples and the question of why she was not recognized.

How will the employee know what to discuss? The job description and/or performance review instrument is the place to start. She can make direct comparisons between competencies/skills and goals, and achievements over the previous year. "The job description says I have to accomplish A, B, and C, and here are examples of my accomplishing A, B, and C." That's a direct, yes or no approach, and it's a good start.

Adding a social recognition dashboard to each employee's tool kit deepens the conversation, because crowdsourced recognition shows what impact the employee has had on her coworkers, internal customers, and others. Preparing for the review, every employee should review the times she has been recognized through the year and apply those moments to the job requirements.

Figure 7.2 on page 151 shows an example from the social recognition record of a project manager named Dana, who works with her manager Liz at Hydrolab, the fictional company introduced in earlier chapters. One of Dana's goals is to lead the prototyping process for new products.

As employees study their recognition moments, they can relate them to specific accomplishments and make a one-to-one comparison to the job description. These moments provide inspiration for the SAR stories that turn the employee's side of the conversation from passive recipient to active participant.

How Managers Prepare

Preparing to assess each employee's performance, manager Liz first focuses on outcomes. That's the highest organization perspective—whether an employee's goals were reached. This is easy with quota-based jobs like sales or quality management and subtler with subjectively judged jobs like training or design.

The degree to which performance is assessed against certain objective targets also depends on company mission and culture. For example, a web design firm might view two iterative, public releases of software in a month as a positive sign of innovation and pushing the competitive envelope. It might regard the speed with which products are released as a metric that is more important than the number of initial flaws. By contrast, a quality-control software firm might view two iterative releases and bug fixes as a branding catastrophe and regard speed of release as nothing compared to 100 percent reliability.

Performance assessment begins with some of those yes/no questions. Did the product ship on time? What is our customer renewal rate? Did our spending stay within budget? Was the open rate on our direct e-mail solicitations 4 percent or above? It's good management practice to apply relevant data wherever possible, and where those data are available, it's a straightforward judgment. The performance criteria tend to flow down from larger company strategies. This is the simple stuff, and performance review instruments are good at registering those yes/no data points.

In practice, a manager like Liz might complete the simple instrument first and then dive into the performance intelligence supplied by social recognition. Or she might alternate between the simple forms and social recognition data as the employee above did. The sequential versus alternating choice is a matter of personal preference; the point is to inform the traditional process with the rich narrative of the crowdsourced data.

As we move from the business metrics to the crowdsourced feedback, we are also moving from evaluating low-level business outcomes to overall cultural fit. The fit with culture and contribution to culture are mostly addressed in this section of the review.

The process of deepening the traditional review with social recognition information is the same for employer and employee up to this point, but here the task diverges. Whereas Dana uses crowdsourced input to trigger a narrative (the SAR stories), Liz uses crowdsourced input to trigger an investigation into the narrative. This is the beginning of understanding not only *what* was accomplished but also *how* it was accomplished and of discovering hidden information that can help performance. (The narrative was "hidden" to Liz, who wasn't always on the scene to witness Dana's behavior. Crowdsourcing's eyewitness input is thus new information that the manager can use in his or her performance assessment.)

After assessing the simple stuff, examine the crowdsourced input on the employee to see where it relates to quantifiable goals. The "regression analysis" that social recognition notations provide can supply additional data for Liz's understanding of how one employee exceeded a quantifiable goal, and another barely made it.

Let's return to Dana's recognition award above, and view the social recognition input from Liz's point of view.

The project management process requires input from many disciplines and departments, none of which report directly to the project manager. A few months ago, three colleagues at Hydrolab recognized Dana's work in moving along the prototype for the GTY project. (See Figure 7.2.)

Quantifying this performance is easy enough: The prototype met a deadline, so Dana "met expectations." In a traditional setting, Liz would check off the box next to the job requirement "hits the deadlines."

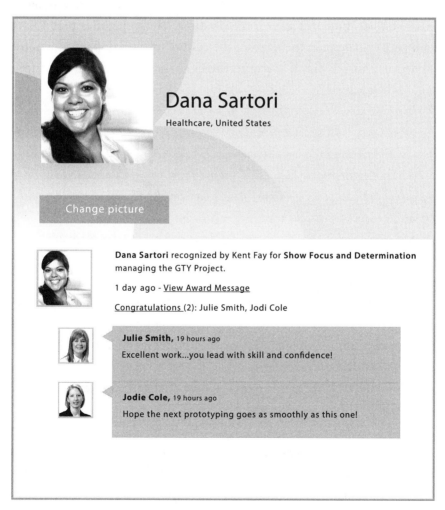

Figure 7.2 Social recognition record for Dana

Anyone who's been in an interdepartmental prototyping process, however, knows that it can be a swamp of miscommunication, infighting, low accountability, crossed lines of authority, and endless rework. You can meet a deadline with nobody left on speaking terms. Yet Dana has obviously done something special: She leads "with skill and confidence." People "hope the next prototyping goes as smoothly as this one." And her initial award is tied to the company value of "show focus and determination," which in this company's lexicon means she is focused, directed, and efficient.

As Liz prepares Dana's performance review, she connects that simple check mark to a broader set of qualities—the very qualities that make it possible to do more than meet the deadline. Those qualities that reflect company values are at the heart of the culture of the company. Liz notes an opportunity to dig deeper into the GTY project during the performance review.

Liz will ask, *"Tell me about the GTY project. What did you do that made it go so smoothly? Was this different from other projects? Can we replicate some new or different technique you used?"*

Dana might reply, *"The GTY project went smoothly because I wrote to the global project managers asking if they had developed similar versions of the product for other clients. We were able to reuse several components that had been developed in the Atlanta office instead of doing that work from the ground up."*

She continues, *"As for the process going smoothly, I also brainstormed with the global PMs about bottlenecks, and headed them off before they happened."*

Now they're having a business conversation. And the organization has learned an improved process that it can propagate throughout the world, magnifying Dana's "small" improvement into a significant improvement; a best practice is born.

How much richer is this than a simple check mark next to "hits the deadlines?"

The Performance Social Graph

After reviewing the factors set out in the job description and/or performance review instrument, the manager has a final, critical subject to study: the context in which the employee functioned. In a traditional review this is typically lumped under a category like "teamwork," or it's a contributing factor in analyzing performance. For example, an employee might have experienced a lot of turnover on her team resulting from restructuring. If she performed well, is that because the team was restructured in a way that made achieving excellence easier, or did she do well in spite of the fact that a restructuring meant she inherited more work from departed colleagues? If she did poorly, was the team restructuring the cause? Since companies are dynamic, factors such as these color performance throughout a business year.

If the manager is diligent, he takes these environmental factors into account, but they fall through the cracks of traditional reviews, again only being mentioned in that vague area called "comments."

What the traditional performance review lacks, social recognition can supply—a real-time *performance social graph.*

A performance social graph renders a picture of the interactions around achievement among employees in a group and beyond. Data visualization is a powerful tool for understanding what has typically remained vague (which is why it is part of most big data initiatives today). Figure 7.3 is a simple visualization of our fictional project manager's performance connections.

This figure shows who has recognized Dana and who has been recognized by her for outstanding work. Now Dana's performance can be seen in a larger context; Liz can visualize team dynamics and heretofore unknown connections. This is bigger than a team and does not rely only on formal reporting structures because these individuals can be anywhere in the company; what matters is that all the people shown are observers of performance and originators of goodwill. This performance social chart is already a snapshot of the Positivity Dominated Workplace.

Dana's network can also be visualized as a series of interactions among all the members giving and receiving awards.

Now Liz can see who is noticing outstanding work among an entire workgroup—who is interacting, who the outliers are, and who is giving and receiving support. Liz can understand the entire dynamic of teamwork in Dana's workgroup.

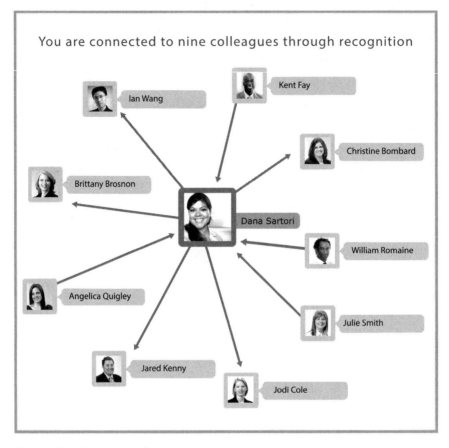

Figure 7.3 Dana's performance connections

This social performance chart (Figure 7.4) shows relationship and connection, and the recognition dashboard provides narrative. This is enough for a rich discussion of Dana's performance, but another visualization of the data invites a review of that vital but hard-to-answer question: Is Dana's performance actually connected to company values?

Each recognition award has been connected to at least one company value. The social recognition system requires everyone to consider how a particular act or accomplishment relates to company culture, and this reinforces the culture. Now Dana's performance review captures her both doing things right (achievement) and doing the right things (culture). Dana and Liz can relate her work directing projects to the reinforcement of that culture, thus propagating the culture while doing the work.

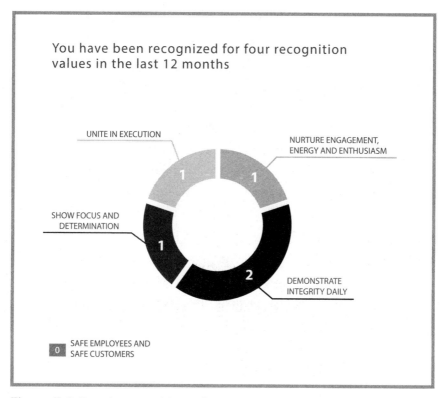

You have been recognized for four recognition values in the last 12 months

UNITE IN EXECUTION

NURTURE ENGAGEMENT, ENERGY AND ENTHUSIASM

SHOW FOCUS AND DETERMINATION

DEMONSTRATE INTEGRITY DAILY

SAFE EMPLOYEES AND SAFE CUSTOMERS

Figure 7.4 Dana's recognition values

Of the five values shown in the performance social chart in Figure 7.4, Dana's awards have mentioned four. She hasn't yet been recognized for Hydrolab's "safe employees and safe customers" value. That might not be relevant to a project manager working in meetings and at a computer all day, but it is a company value and its absence is also worth discussing. If Dana were an installer of Hydrolab equipment at a client site, this might be a red flag. Maybe this is of little consequence to Dana and Liz, but it can also spark brainstorming about how she might contribute to the "safe employees and safe customers" imperative. (Or, Dana might be making extra efforts to promote safety without anyone—including her manager—recognizing it. The manager should take note.)

I've said that a self-perpetuating culture is the holy grail of performance management; so connecting these values to specific achievements helps to build that in the minds and behaviors of employee and manager alike.

Social recognition data visualization thus adds insight to the processes, personalities, and dynamics that encourage the right behaviors. The manager has moved far beyond simply deciding if a goal was met to understanding how it was met.

Managers learn which employees are most engaged in their work and visualize how company goals and values are being lived in day-to-day behavior. If over time all the recognition moments are captured in a smart database, social recognition and the traditional review together show the organizational forces that influence performance. This empowers the manager to do one of his or her most important jobs: remove roadblocks to progress and smooth the path to achievement for any employee with the skills and willingness to excel.

Combine the Best of the Traditional and Crowdsourced Reviews

Both employee and manager at this point have reviewed written and visual data recounting the employee's achievement. They are now ready for that business conversation that goes way beyond the "state, rate, and comment" routine I mention earlier.

The final format for the discussion depends partly on company policy and formal performance review instruments, whether those are on paper, online, or in another form. Differences notwithstanding, here are the ways in which both parties can use crowdsourced social recognition to reach the goal: a performance review in which the manager fully understands, describes, and enhances the employee's performance, yesterday and in the future. (The following examples use our fictional Dana and her manager, Liz, as well as the names of their peers at Hydrolab.)

1. *Restate the purpose of the review and confirm that both parties are ready.* Most employees feel at least some anxiety, or at least anticipation, at the outset. The manager can repeat the purpose of the review, its scope, and the hoped-for outcome. Confirm that both employee

and manager are prepared. Depending on the company's format, the employee might have seen the completed review in advance (HR experts suggest this method, in the spirit of "no surprises" and to give either disappointed or excited feelings a chance to settle, to encourage that detached "business conversation" tone.)

LIZ: *Dana, even though we talk all through the year about our work, this is a time reserved to discuss in depth how you've performed in your job over the last year, what you think your strengths are, and where you might want to develop or stretch your skills. You've seen both the performance review sheet and the social recognition dashboard, right? [Confirmed.] Great. Let's start by going through the formal stuff line by line, and go deeper wherever we feel we should.*

2. *Review the performance assessment and social recognition together.* As employee and manager work through the performance review's formal instrument, they should return to any of the recognition events that pertain to the skill or goal being discussed. This allows the manager to ask questions she's prepared; offer praise, encouragement, or advice; and raise potential issues. The employee can help the analysis by telling the SAR-structured stories she's prepared. If there is disagreement about the proficiency rating, this is a time to open a discussion of those issues because both parties are dealing with facts and real events.

LIZ: *Getting the project managers to share components of client products was a brilliant idea. Of course lots of this work is interchangeable, but it took someone in your position to make the most of assets we already had. I'm curious, though—did our developers resist using components that were built in another office? They have to guarantee the quality of the work for the client.*

DANA: *That's why I built time in the schedule for the software components to go to quality assurance first. It's just a prototype for the client to see, so we didn't have to worry about perfection but we had to get the look-and-feel factors right. The result of using Atlanta's work and running it through QA first saved our developers a couple of days on the schedule.*

LIZ: *And I see how that rings the "work with purpose" bell that your recognition award shows. Changing the process while delivering the prototype on time was exactly the efficiency we expect in project management, and this is a great example. Between that and your other work I'm comfortable with this "exceeds expectations" rating.*

DANA: *Great—me too!*

3. *Compare achievements to goals.* To the degree the traditional performance review instrument allows, the manager and employee should compare actual achievements (deliverables, quotas, etc.) to goals that were established at the last review or that appear in the job description. This might simply be a comparison between goals and reality; for example, "85 percent of projects completed on time." However, if the job or business conditions have changed over the year (as discussed in Chapter 1), social recognition's narrative power can be particularly helpful at this point.

DANA: *We discussed the fact that a lot of project work landed on my desk after Robert left for Chicago. He tried to tie things up, but I'm hoping that you get authorization to replace him soon.*

LIZ: *I saw that you, Amy, and James all finished up Robert's projects, and I was glad to award you for the extra effort. I've also made a point of mentioning your extraordinary extra effort in the award, and the last time I met with Trevor he remarked on it. I know it took a lot of extra effort, especially since we've got a slow—well, deliberate—hiring process here. I think we'll have someone in Robert's seat within three weeks. Tell me more about this—is the workload too much for any of you? Can Robert's projects still be delivered on time?*

DANA: *The workload isn't overwhelming now, but pushing two of his projects along with mine doesn't give me bandwidth for much else. I did appreciate the recognition for taking on his work, and I was really gratified that so many people congratulated me on the award.*

There were even notes from people I've never met but only knew through e-mail.

LIZ: *It was well deserved. We'll get Robert's replacement here soon.*

4. *Discuss how business goals and dynamics relate to the employee's performance.* The last dialogue dealt with a simple change in the office: a project manager left and hasn't been replaced yet. Recognition and the manager's plans to address the situation play into the conversation. Now is a good time to review any significant changes in the business in the past year, in part because of the deeper view it gives performance and in part because it sets up the forward-looking close of the review. It's a time to list changes and probe for commentary on how they affect the employee's ability to do her job.

Changes might include restructuring, personnel changes, crises of various kinds, shifting priorities (for example, a sudden need to face a competitive threat or a need to cut costs quickly). Changes are not all negative: The company might see an opportunity and move quickly to exploit it.

LIZ: *You helped members of the training staff about six months ago when they were teaching Hydrolab's project management system to the Chicago office. Now that the corner office folks have announced the acquisition of GeoClean, how would you like to have a more formal role in integrating the company's systems? Your initiative with the Atlanta development group on GTY makes me think you could take a lead role in that. It would go beyond just teaching, and you'd get in front of the strategic business team. I think it's time to raise your profile.*

DANA: *That sounds amazing! Tell me more about what that would require.*

Social recognition can support this kind of dynamic change and supplements the traditional performance review's inability to change at the speed of business. If not for the award, Dana's extraordinary effort might not have been discussed because taking over for Robert wasn't part of her objectives—objectives that were formalized the previous January.

Since the vast majority of employees fall somewhere on the scale between superior and incompetent, most performance reviews will deal with that middle 70 percent of performance. How might they distinguish themselves? For lots of competent, loyal, and proficient employees, just accomplishing the job is plenty of work. Moreover, interdependent work makes it hard to know how much to credit personal initiative and how much to credit the power of teamwork.

For that matter, how can a manager credit individual employees for the achievement of shared goals?

This is where social recognition can address questions of attribution in a creative way. For example, a company might set a goal of cutting energy costs by 12 percent in a year. Saving energy is everyone's job! Since everyone is using energy, how can a legitimate metric apply to this goal? Should this appear somehow on a performance review in a quantifiable way? Ultimately, the company will know if it's saved energy this year. Short of putting an electric meter on everyone's desktop, how can people be judged on this initiative in a performance review?

Most employees probably can't be judged on this goal in a uniform, quantifiable way, but social recognition allows additional initiative, innovative ideas, or "extra mile" behaviors for saving energy to be noted—and that can go into a person's performance review. This is that elusive spirit of engagement made public. Imagine that employees named Brendan and Shauna in accounts payable make a game out of an "energy audit" in the department, confirming that everyone's computer is in sleep mode after ten minutes of activity. Nobody anticipated that need, and it's not in anyone's yearly goals, but lots of their peers will recognize the extra effort and creativity. Recognition can occupy the space between formal goals.

5. *Take time for open-ended discussion.* Listening with an open mind might be the least-used technique of the traditional performance review. Perhaps because the traditional tone is one of the manager handing down a judgment, both parties habitually rely on the list of

skills or goals on the performance instrument. We've already seen how relating recognition moments to the job description allows a richer picture of performance to emerge. Now, late in the review, is the time for the manager to ask some open-ended questions. They might come from the manager's preparation, but often they come from the business conversation that crowdsourced performance reviews can be. A manager might ask, for example, if there are skills or training the employee feels would be helpful for her growth. So ask, and allow a little time for the employee to answer. (If she asks, "What do you mean?" as many will, offer a suggestion or two and again, be silent.)

Were attributes or skills that are not in the job description called out in crowdsourced information? Do they in fact belong in the job description or the performance review going forward? The recrafting of performance expectations, inspired by social recognition, is a great benefit of the crowdsourced review. New attributes must of course be directly related to the job and relatable to company values.

Team dynamics are important to explore in an open-ended talk, and social recognition data can inspire some otherwise forgotten observations. This is because recognition by its nature arises from relationships. Manager and employee can talk about what corporate values the employee was recognized for, and what's missing. Talk about what connections have appeared outside the immediate group, both to and from the employee. Sometimes people who work five floors apart interact more than they do with a neighbor ten feet away, and that cross-departmental connection is part of the social architecture. Manager and employee can see these deep connections through social recognition, whereas before they might have been invisible. And they can learn how these connections can be leveraged to improve overall performance.

Open-ended discussion can reveal easily mended gaps in the employee's tool kit. Can she relate her work to overall budgets, revenue, and company business lines? Since social recognition uses the language of company values, you might ask the employee to relate in her own words how her work applies to any of the values.

This is also a good place in the interview to ask about awards the employee has given. Is she participating in the social recognition program? Is she fully informed about the nature of the jobs around her (social recognition relies on some knowledge of a recipient's work)? How are the social recognition program and the performance review system informing her about her priorities for the year to come?

> LIZ: *Can you think of anything you need that we haven't discussed?*
>
> DANA: *If I help with the integration of GeoClean, do you think I'll need to know more about how to read financial data? Profit and loss statements and all that?*
>
> LIZ: *That's a good question. I don't think you'll need that to do the work, but it might be good to get you some basics before the GeoClean integration project turns strategic. It certainly is a good area to know as you move up. I'll make a note to talk with HR about the online training we have to find out if there are some options.*

6. *End the meeting with a forward-looking discussion.* After both parties believe they've covered any open matters, they should close the meeting with a one- or two-sentence review of the overall performance. Assuming that this review has not been combined with a promotion, change of title, or lateral move (and they are only occasionally part of a review), they should close with a forward-looking review of the next year. In many traditional systems, this is the point at which the manager shows the goals and expectations for the coming year. In others, that's a separate discussion. Either way, the end of the meeting connects past performance with what's coming up. I say more about plans for developing and/or improving performance in Chapter 8.

> DANA: *I'm glad to see that we agree on the quality of my work, and I'm looking forward to that integration project. It's good to know Robert's replacement is coming soon. I think the company is doing a great job*

with the product line, and I'm hoping to bring more initiatives like the Atlanta idea to you soon.

LIZ: *Dana, just like Julie said in the GTY award, your confidence is inspiring to the newer people in this group. I think of you as a leader among the managers, and while the regular work has to get done, and you do it very, very well, I'm looking forward to seeing you in a more public role going forward.*

Discussing Money, Perks, Benefits, and Promotions

Most HR departments I know advise managers to make discussions of money, perks, and benefits separate from the formal performance review. The reason is that most managers don't have a lot of leeway when it comes to distributing raises among staff members—typically just a few percentage points. HR departments are in charge of benefits, and equity among employees forms policies like how much vacation time an employee has earned.

The less obvious reason is that an effective performance review is focused on performance not just reward, and while the two are obviously linked, money can be a distraction crowding out other issues.

Compensation news can be confided to the employee separately in the context of overall company performance as well as individual merit. Bonuses that a manager might have more flexibility in awarding should be connected to performance, but again, in the context of budgets, overall performance and the employee's potential as well as performance. (Some HR departments differ on this and ultimately how you talk about money is a cultural issue in companies, as it is in families and even countries.)

There are two obvious exceptions to this policy. Commissions, special incentives, and other performance-based cash rewards, typically offered in sales, are so intimately tied to performance they can be discussed but they follow a departmental formula, so the math dictates the amount, not the manager's opinion. Money awarded in a social recognition program is similar—it follows a preplanned formula. And because social recognition awards are given throughout the year, employees know what they've earned before the day of the review.

The second exception might be a performance review that concludes with the good news that the employee is being promoted. These are usually the times compensation takes a jump, and HR and managers understand that when you tell someone she's being promoted or moving laterally to take on a new assignment, you have to address what it means to her compensation.

Performance from a Team Perspective

Separate from the individual performance review but intimately related is that managers can gain a perspective on team performance and team dynamics using social recognition data.

Dana is not only a project manager, but she also manages a team. In the performance social chart of her system (Figure 7.5), she can see details of how her staff interacts with each other and the rest of the company by showing the connections among them via recognition.

HR leaders can see how many people have been recognized and for what. For example, the company value of "show focus and determination" is a popular award, so Dana knows she's getting her message across *and so does her manager.* It's a great value for project managers, as is "unite in execution" because these are critical attributes of project management. Both Dana and Liz can visualize how she's balancing the various values and ways of working that flow from Hydrolab's stated values. They can also see that 20 percent of Dana's team has not participated in social recognition, which raises the question of why not? Now that Dana sees that, she can investigate whether there's a problem. Maybe someone doesn't understand the system, or maybe someone isn't being recognized at all. Both possibilities call for action. Liz can see Dana's individual dashboard, her team's dashboard, and that of every other manager she supervises. She can survey social recognition over time, say the previous 12 months, and get a general sense of some demographic award activities of values

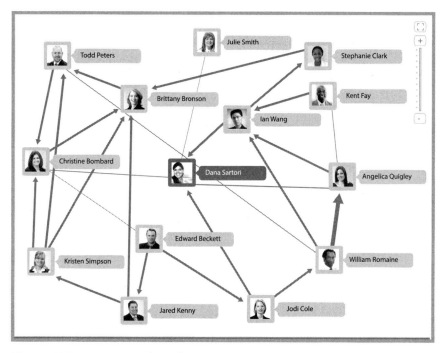

Figure 7.5 Dana's social performance

given and received. Liz and Dana can zoom in on a team or an individual, study the individual instances of recognition, and bring that information to the performance discussion both in terms of the individual and in terms of team dynamics.

Any skilled manager knows that individuals count and also that how teams work can make or break individual performance. Visualizing the team's interactions, communications, and expressions of company values gives a supervisor the information he or she needs to create a high-performing team.

What About Negative Feedback?

Management 101 advises, "Praise in public, criticize in private." And the performance review is a private conversation between employee and supervisor. To this point I've focused on the positive, professional exploration that a business conversation like a performance review should be.

Alas, there is also a need in business for negative feedback. Managers who shy away from delivering bad news or model their reviews on the old "performance review sandwich" of positive-negative-positive comments, risk their team's performance by allowing a problem to go unresolved.

The coaching that is part of every manager's job includes setting expectations and enforcing them. Constructive criticism, done right, is part of a good performance review. This is best handled in traditional review format, not through social recognition. HR must continue to teach managers to notice subpar performance and lead employees to improve. And just like positive feedback, negative feedback should be timely and given as soon as possible to the event or situation that causes it. Don't wait until the annual review for corrective action.

Here's a question I get only from HR industry analysts: "Shouldn't social recognition also give negative feedback?" HR field practitioners never ask this question, but it comes up enough in the industry to warrant an answer: Negative feedback has no place in social recognition.

Why not? Shouldn't a manager be able to say, "Hey, you really screwed up in that situation?" Wouldn't it be interesting to have everyone noticing bad performance as well as good? What if you could deduct dollars from someone's bonus when he or she makes a mistake? Wouldn't those data be interesting?

> *Negative feedback has no place in social recognition.*

I answer that, well, *all* data are interesting, but when you talk to our customers, the HR people, and managers who keep companies running, they all have an allergic reaction to negative recognition. It introduces a toxic element to a culture you're trying to nurture. It's much akin to the problems of the compliment sandwich: "Great job, Joe, but if you'd done the middle task better, the client would be happier. But overall, you do good work." At best, this confuses the recipient. Did Joe do a good job or not? At worst, it alienates and demotivates.

Ultimately you want a social recognition system to relentlessly shine a light on positive behaviors and positive outcomes. Consider current software trends in which tools and systems are disaggregated and specialized—think of apps rather than huge suites of software—so they accomplish exactly what they are meant to accomplish. Mixing "constructive criticism" in a system intended to power up culture sends conflicting messages.

HR practitioners know that company culture is fragile and can easily be killed. And thinking about the wisdom of crowds, do you really want to give an "atomic culture bomb" to everyone in your company? Social recognition is by its nature public. Keep it positive, and you'll get positive outcomes. A recognition program is not the place to give negative feedback because it's a toxic influence on behavior. The recognition program is focused entirely on creating a Positivity Dominated Workplace.

The New York Times columnist David Brooks, who often dives deep into sociology, noted, "The way to get someone out of a negative cascade is not with a ferocious email trying to attack their bad behavior. It's to go on the offense and try to maximize some alternative good behavior. There's a trove of research suggesting that it's best to tackle negative behaviors obliquely by redirecting attention toward different, positive behaviors."[3] Social recognition, social architecture, and the tools of a crowdsourced performance review *do* have a role in improving performance, however. We all have the capacity to improve, if we're properly led, coached, and rewarded. How to make that happen is the subject of the next chapter.

8 | Improving Performance After the Review

To an outsider, Tony could resemble a cartoon version of a software engineer: quiet, intense, bearded, and wearing the uniform of jeans and a T-shirt most days at work. He kept to himself, rarely going out with peers after work and rarely speaking up in meetings.

Liz had always suspected that there was more to Tony than the two-dimensional nerd image. She sensed potential leadership in him, and she had looked for evidence that he could be more than a single contributor.

Liz found her answer in the social recognition platform, where others had revealed the hidden benefit of his intensity. On Tony's social recognition platform, peers and managers had consistently noted that Tony's perfectionism led him to insist that the software code be "elegant" as well as effective. Once, Tony had volunteered to review the code of a less experienced engineer. That engineer had awarded Tony his only recognition based on the Hydrolab value, "taking action together."

Now Liz was ready to challenge Tony to use his perfectionism in a more public way. In his performance review, she said, "Tony, your independence is part of your value, and yet I think that others in the group could benefit from your experience. Are there ways you might tackle your work more in partnership with others?"

Tony shrugged, but looked at his social graph on Liz's computer screen. "What do you mean by partnership?"

"Your social connections are strong within the group. I can see that by the recognition awards you've given and received. I understand that you like to work mostly on your own, but how might our value of taking action together be more a part of your work? How can we expand your sphere of influence outside the department?"

"When you say outside, do you mean like, with the sales and marketing people?" Tony asked. He looked dubious.

Liz laughed, "No, not them. I'm thinking of the global integration challenges we're about to face with a new team of developers. I'd like you to join Dana on the GeoClean acquisition integration team."

"What would I do?" asked Tony.

"What you do now," Liz replied. "Make sure the code coming from GeoClean is elegant."

What causes a person to improve job performance?

The *least* powerful creator of change is coercion from the boss. "Improve or else" is the subtext of many traditional performance reviews, but HR case studies (as well as common experience) show that the manager who "forces" better performance hurts productivity in the long run. Employees thus motivated to change are not attached to the job through internal or social gratification, but change only because of *fear*. That might work in a sweatshop, but not in a modern business.

At the opposite extreme, the urge to improve can come entirely from the employee herself. It might take the form of ambition to grow and take on new challenges. The urge to improve for self-actualization is the purest fire. Executives who manage people so driven are lucky, and their job is to guide and direct that fire.

Between the extremes of coercion and self-actualization, the influence of friends, family, coworkers, and other peers is a cheap, renewable source of employee energy. When employees believe that the team's success benefits all, they cheer each other on (and pressure underperformers to improve). The motivational power of moving from "me" to "us" drives success in team efforts from start-up companies to sports teams. The manager who makes such teams possible is harnessing the power of social rewards among her employees.

There's also pay for performance: Improve and get a raise. Money is the most commonly applied motivator for employees, and its power is real but limited by budgetary constraints, salary bands, and business conditions. A raise tends to normalize and lose impact ("whatever you pay, in six months it won't be enough"). Compared to self-actualization from within, money has to be constantly resubmitted as a motivator. And money is the easiest tool for a competitor to use to lure an outstanding employee away. So while compensation is part of the equation, money alone is a less-than-perfect instrument for improving performance.

This leaves a manager with these options for improving performance during and after the review:

1. Coerce improvement based on authority (weak).
2. Hire only self-motivated people (rare).
3. Achieve improvement with monetary and material rewards (temporary).
4. Nurture a Positivity Dominated Workplace and constant improvement (ideal).

The crowdsourced performance review inspires the last option. What follows are ways to apply its tenets to encourage a culture of constant improvement among your employees. Whether you discuss these principles in the review or not, you should apply them throughout the work year because they create continuous, incremental improvements—the kind that become permanent.

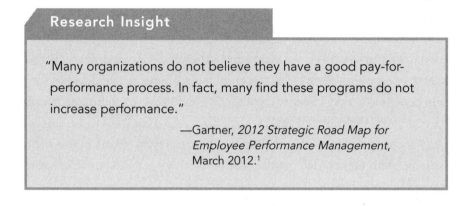

Research Insight

"Many organizations do not believe they have a good pay-for-performance process. In fact, many find these programs do not increase performance."

—Gartner, *2012 Strategic Road Map for Employee Performance Management*, March 2012.[1]

Growing a Job

In the fictional dialogues in Chapter 7, manager Liz used crowdsourced feedback and social recognition to highlight an employee's achievements. Social recognition contributes to a conversation about areas for improvement as well.

When it comes to improving performance, social recognition conforms to the advice of management thinkers like Peter Drucker, who believed that the way to great performance is to focus most work time on strengths. Yes, improvement does mean filling some gaps (in knowledge, or changing an attitude), and the positivity of social recognition drives change by inspiring a person to grow.

A manager must ask, what is the crowd saying about the employee's work? Does the employee agree with that assessment? Social recognition is positive by definition, so this conversation can be positive, and in that spirit the manager can probe a little deeper. Why was a strength or behavior recognized? Why did the employee behave that way?

For example, looking at an employee's performance social graph, software engineering manager Liz might see that employee Tony has been recognized for his drive to deliver quality work. The crowd notes that, even when "good" is sufficient, this employee insists on "perfect" or "awesome" as the only acceptable outcome. Tony's an introverted fellow, quietly urging the team to do better, never blowing his own horn but remaining with the job until it approaches perfection.

How might Liz respond to such strength? With congratulations, certainly, and a high rating in Tony's performance review. She can then go further and talk with Tony about adding or spearheading a quality target for the whole group as part of his performance goals for the next year. His quiet influence on the group has now become a shared asset and part of his performance review.

As Tony's recognition for boosting quality among his peers continues, other metrics measuring quality of the group's work can be tracked simultaneously, and the relationship between the numbers can be analyzed. The definition of quality varies with the job, but metrics are available in every discipline, from handling customer calls to creating spreadsheets to reducing downtime in an assembly process to rolling installation trucks.

I caution you that social recognition and traditional output measurements do not rigidly march in lockstep because recognition is a cultural act taking place in the realm of values and is not an automatic and fully quantifiable output. *Recognition is, like engagement, energy, and creativity, measurable but is about more than a single metric. Recognition powers culture, and that culture delivers improved business metrics.*

> *Recognition is, like engagement, energy, and creativity, measurable but is about more than a single metric.*

Dealing with Gaps in Recognition

How do social recognition data relate to performance metrics? Because social recognition is positive and depends on voluntary participation, we know that its presence on someone's record indicates accomplishment. Relating that to specific values, projects, and tasks makes the connection.

Let's return to the fictional company Hydrolab, whose recognition values are the following:

- Safe employees and safe customers
- Show focus and determination.
- Demonstrate integrity daily.
- Nurture engagement, energy and enthusiasm.
- Unite in execution.

Tony's insistence on quality has been recognized by his peers chiefly in the values of "show focus and determination," "demonstrate integrity daily," and once for "unite in execution." Once, he was recognized in the value "safe employees and safe customers," but that value doesn't have much bearing on his desk job. As an introvert, Tony doesn't show a lot of emotion around "nurture engagement, energy and enthusiasm." (See Figure 8.1.)

Tony's manager Liz might be concerned about his relatively low recognition in "nurture engagement, energy and enthusiasm," but she realizes that this might just reflect Tony's temperament. As a conscientious manager she'll ask about that word "inspiration" with questions like these:

"Tony, I know you like to work on your own, and you focus on getting things perfect. One of the values Hydrolab stresses is nurturing engagement, energy, and enthusiasm in our work. Do you think you can say that about your job? If not, are there changes we might make that might make you feel more excited and engaged? I'm impressed by the influence you have on the team in terms of raising overall quality. Do you see other potential improvements you'd like to take on?"

"I'd like to talk about how we unite in execution in our department. Do you understand why that value can be important in this particular work? Let's consider what work is best done alone and what might benefit from greater teamwork."

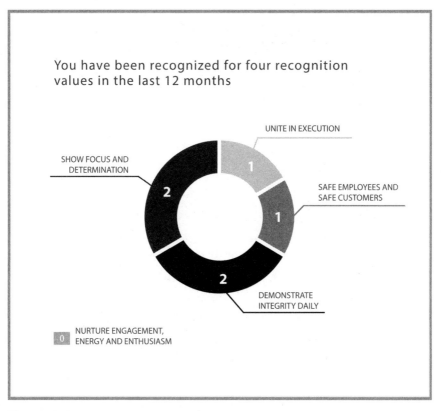

Figure 8.1 Tony's recognition values

Liz is coaching Tony, which is how she helps raise performance. Conversations such as these can take place during or outside the performance review. They are inspired by recognition's ability to reveal the social graph of today's interdependent workplace.

When Recognition Is Absent

What if an employee doesn't receive social recognition? This calls for inquiry because it can reveal benign, moderate, or destructive situations. Social recognition in this context can act as a kind of early-warning system, or it might simply confirm what is already suspected. Social and cultural causes can include:

- *Isolation*: Certain jobs might have little contact with others, like the remote worker mentioned in Chapter 1. It's up to the isolated employee's manager to recognize accomplishment and strengthen social ties. She also should encourage those whose work is affected by the isolated employee to recognize accomplishment thus making it visible.

- *Weak social ties*: Some transitional situations, such as a group of temporary workers brought in to handle a seasonal workload, discourage long-term social interactions. Widely decentralized teams also have less interaction (although this doesn't stop JetBlue from social recognition, as we saw in Chapter 5). In these cases, management must weigh the benefits of building stronger social ties in the short term with a recognition program or a structure that capitalizes on existing social ties. Sometimes a large company will contract retired employees to handle a seasonal surge of work, knowing that their collective knowledge and long-standing bonds of social cohesion made them incredibly productive.

- *Social discomfort or dysfunction*: We all know that workplaces can be the scene of rivalries, dysfunctional social dynamics like harassment, and/or outright hostility. These conditions indicate a toxic culture that calls for strong executive action. While social recognition can certainly be part of a solution, it must be implemented as part of a larger cultural overhaul. Sometimes these pernicious problems are limited to an individual, department, office, or division, and social recognition reveals the problem. For example, if one department deviates widely from the company norm in recognizing "working together." HR and leadership should find out why and hold the leader accountable.

- *Slow implementation*: It's possible that the implementation of social recognition in a department or office has faltered. Check participation levels against companywide participation, and if people aren't using the program, find out why. (See also the Appendix, "Implementing Social Recognition.")

Encouraging Personal Growth

The performance review envisioned in Chapter 7 concludes with a discussion about expectations for the coming months and year. That conversation should continue throughout the year in the spirit of continuous growth and improvement of the employee's performance. Social recognition creates milestones for that conversation between formal performance reviews.

First, every recognition moment invites congratulations and thanks. Employee engagement surveys tell us that these simple acts have great impact. Employees feel validated, respected, and appreciated in the context of company values.

This change is tangible: Within three months of embarking on its recognition platform (called Lift), an internal monthly JetBlue survey revealed an 88 percent increase in crew member satisfaction with respect to rewards and recognition associated with positive behaviors.

Recognition moments also invite "instant analysis" for an individual and his team. Ask an employee to tell a story. For a manager, this conversation can sound a little like behavior-based job interviewing. "Hey Tony, tell me about that project. What made it go so smoothly?" Remember that work is a narrative, and the message you gave last week and last month is best enforced today not by you but by personal testimony and self-reflection. Incidentally, recognition moments enrich these conversations because they are genuine and unforced. The manager is talking about a real event, not an abstract concept. For those managers whose style is not given to random acts of support, social recognition supplies the timing.

> *For those managers whose style is not given to random acts of support, social recognition supplies the timing.*

Encourage each employee to recognize the work of others. Recognition is voluntary and thus is not appropriate as a job requirement, but for all the reasons I've discussed, it is a positive contribution any employee can make to better performance in others. A Positivity Dominated Workplace magnifies energy and engagement because giving recognition requires one to ask, "How does this person's actions benefit the company and further our work?" In this sense, everyone in a Positivity Dominated Workplace becomes a strategic thinker. The power to recognize a peer confers efficacy on even the greenest entry-level employee.

Performance Management and Career Paths

Great managers know that a high-performing work group is dynamic. People join, do great work, and then move on, up, or out. HR professionals plan career paths with the strongest workers so that they stay with the company when they have outgrown their jobs. Workforce management pros also know that career path planning is as individual as each worker—everyone has a unique mix of ambition, mobility, motivation, and desire to grow.

Career path planning is part of performance management. People are motivated by progress and are eager to see it. This naturally pertains to the high-potential and high-performing individuals, and in a strong company culture they get mentoring, career direction, and opportunities to excel. They are offered the chance to take on greater risk and reward. Their obvious high performance tends to earn them recognition by employees and peers.

Recognition for these high achievers functions as one measure of their impact, wherever they sit in the hierarchy. For them, recognition may be thought of as a tool of insight into development—what do people say about their accomplishments? What conversations about their impact might recognition start? And in planning their careers within the company, what strengths do recognition data reveal and where do they need reinforcement? With greater performance comes greater expectation, and so for example, what might be a minor flaw in an average performer—say, little ability to inspire enthusiastic engagement in projects—might be a performance killer once someone rises to manage a large team.

Social recognition can also inform the progress of individuals belonging to that indispensible "middle 70 percent" of employees whose skills, energy, and commitment fuel the company's success. These too are cultural energizers because they inspire those around them with their attitude. While organizations naturally lavish attention on their top performers, social recognition can point out these unsung heroes, mapping their influence on peers that might otherwise go unnoticed.

Preparing for the Unexpected

Business changes so fast these days that you can expect the unexpected to happen. New opportunities appear, crises befall an industry or an economy, key people leave, management changes, and strategy shifts in response to competitive threats. Resilient organizations employ people who respond to changing conditions with equanimity. Great organizations employ people who respond to changing conditions with excitement and energy.

How can this become part of performance management? How can a manager write the unexpected into a job description or a performance review's "expectations" section?

The simple answer is, she can't, and she doesn't have to. If the right people are in place and the right systems adjust to changing conditions, crisis becomes opportunity.

A sturdy job performance system responds to change by setting new goals and by measuring peoples' response to change. Social recognition is the tool to use for that measurement because it operates right at the point of performance, no matter how conditions change. It also is operated by the crowd, and its inclusiveness makes it the perfect tool for making a tactical change in direction.

Let's say Hydrolab sees a brilliant new technology in a small-start up and buys the company with the intention of integrating that technology into its product line. The opportunity window is small, and everyone from engineers to installers to market analysts to financial people to facilities managers—in fact, everyone—contributes to the success of this unexpected opportunity. In a Positivity Dominated Workplace, the attitude is, "Let's all pitch in and do it together!"

Nobody has time to rewrite job descriptions or performance expectations and in a modern organization nobody should. Instead, executives, managers, and line workers mobilize around the opportunity by rewriting task lists, making new relationships and researching new markets, and bearing down on a thousand new tasks.

> *Day by day, a new narrative appears in the social recognition system, expressing the energy and joy of a group working as one.*

Imagine if social recognition is going on throughout this process. People are cheering one another along. They are thanking each other for extra effort, for catching potential disasters before they happen, and for adjusting to the exciting new reality. New relationships appear on the social graph. Day by day, a new narrative appears in the social recognition system, with accomplishments still expressing company values and now expressing the energy and joy of a group working as one. Acts of recognition large and small reinforce camaraderie under pressure. Social cohesion compensates for late nights, big risks, and stressful effort. Executives thank receptionists. The new kid in package design recognizes Margaret in finance for her help, kidding that art and accounting are finally working together. The lab equipment installer in Kansas City recognizes the HR director who flew in from company headquarters just to thank everyone in person for bearing up under the extra workload. And the opportunity reveals a performance culture that is the envy of lesser organizations.

PART 3 THE FUTURE OF PERFORMANCE MANAGEMENT

Big Data, Crowdsourcing, and the Future of HR

Rebecca stood next to a screen in the big conference room, where Hydrolab's directors gathered for their quarterly meeting.

"Turning to the GeoClean acquisition integration, I'm happy to say the employees who came from GeoClean have overcome their doubts about the crowdsourced performance review process. At the time of acquisition, 68 percent of former GeoClean employees expressed a neutral or 'somewhat concerned' attitude toward receiving some of their pay and much of their performance input based on social recognition. A year later, those numbers have flipped: 86 percent are somewhat or very enthusiastic about the system."

"That includes the managers," Rebecca said. "Among the employees who were here before the GeoClean merger, approval of crowdsourcing the performance review is almost 90 percent."

She changed the slide and continued, "Trevor, do you want to speak to this next section?"

Trevor gestured to the screen. "Sure. You're about to see more data about human behavior than you ever thought possible in a company. We have a series of dashboards measuring who is engaged, who is participating, and who is improving their safety and teamwork and focus. Rebecca or I can dial up details about actual work activity, and when you compare it to other results, including the financials in the next section, you'll be amazed at what we've been missing all these years.

"For example, you'll see that the great majority of recognition awards are for small dollar values, which is as it should be. We're getting constant activity around each of the five core values, and awareness of those values among former GeoClean employees is very high. We can measure that, and we can understand why this acquisition is such a success. Morale is good, attrition among the people we hoped to keep is low, and that's reflected in the numbers. The merger went off very well indeed.

"How often does that happen?" Trevor asked. "Rarely. Anyone want to hazard a guess why the GeoClean integration is working so well?"

"You're going to tell us that culture is king," said a director.

"I don't have to tell you that, Bob," Trevor said with a smile. "You wouldn't be here unless you believed it too."

In 2002, Oakland Athletics manager Billy Beane built a winning baseball team despite having the second-smallest budget in the big leagues. He did it by defying time-honored beliefs about which players win baseball games. Rich teams always scooped up the big hitters and lightning-fast pitchers Beane couldn't afford because those superstars, went conventional wisdom, led teams to the World Series. Instead, Beane tunneled into detailed player data and found unglamorous player statistics (such as base-on-balls) that led him to hire underrated players. He changed players' positions, for example making a catcher into a first baseman. The next year, Oakland played beyond all expectations and in 2004 Beane's story was made famous by Michael Lewis's bestselling *Moneyball*[1] (the book and the film that followed).

Here is what Michael Lewis discovered: Billy Beane used data to uncover hidden and untapped potential. Other managers and baseball scouts relied on conventional wisdom, ignoring evidence of certain players' potential to contribute to a winning team. They neglected key statistics, and the tendency of big-spending, big-city teams to win confirmed their prejudices. Until Beane's data-driven analysis, good players were ignored or underused.

Beane was so successful that other managers adopted his methods (and continued to spend big). Now baseball managers scrutinize data the way statisticians do. In other games from poker to football, sweeping data analysis is creating a new generation of experts skilled at applying previously neglected information.

Some of your employees are like those ballplayers that Beane discovered. They are talented and productive, but their value is partially hidden. Sometimes they labor in an obscure spot; sometimes their managers are the "single point of failure" in performance management mentioned in Chapter 1. And sometimes they're just in the wrong job.

These employees represent untapped potential that could make the team better if only it were recognized.

The 2012 U.S. election provided another fascinating window into the potential of both reinterpreting data without prejudice and crowdsourcing.

Nate Silver, a statistician who made an early reputation with innovative models analyzing baseball players, went on to devise a complex statistical model analyzing U.S. political contests. By the time his political blog was acquired by *The New York Times*, Silver's statistical model predicted the outcomes of 2008's presidential and senatorial races with uncanny accuracy. In 2012, well-known traditional polls deviated significantly from Silver's predictions, and yet on November 6 he did it again. Silver called the winner of every state in the presidential contest and 32 of 33 senate contests; no national poll or televised pundit matched his data-driven accuracy.

On the crowdsourcing front, the Internet betting site Intrade.com was nearly as accurate. Intrade sets odds on political contests not with detailed data but by setting each candidate as a metaphorical "stock" that can be bought and sold by people who play the Intrade market. Just like the stock market, the relative value of a candidate is a prediction of his or her future value, for example, his or her chance of winning. The market of traders operates as a crowd—many individuals make judgments about candidates, and their aggregate judgment is the prediction.

The crowdsourced Intrade predictions picked the presidential winner in 49 states and picked the winner in 31 of 33 senate contests, an accuracy rate of 98 and 93 percent, respectively.

Predictive models like Silver's, and crowdsourced predictive markets like Intrade, have a lot to teach us about performance management. Ultimately, a company's data about employees are meant to predict things that will happen in the future, making good performance happen more often and faster and mitigating poor performance by preventing it in the first place.

Predicting behavior by gathering and interpreting the right information is the great promise of data and social recognition.

Diving into Data

Silver wrote an excellent book about predictions called *The Signal and the Noise*,[2] in which he makes three points about using data that I believe are relevant to performance management. Here they are, with my interpretation for human resources.

- *Not all data are equally relevant or related:* An employee's output can be measured, but only certain measurements might be relevant to her performance. For example, one employee might answer 400 customer e-mail inquiries a day with a routine message directing customers to a web "help" site. Another might answer just 30 e-mails a day with detailed help. It's unclear which is more productive because the only measure that matters is how many customers quickly resolved their problem. (Silver also comments that precision of measurement is not the only factor in success. You can precisely measure the wrong data and go far off course.)

- *Unconscious bias distorts analysis:* Performance reviews, like economic and political predictions, tend to gather data that confirm the reviewer's model or prejudged conclusion. If a manager believes an employee is energetic and engaged, he will tend to notice behavior that confirms that belief and disregard contrary behavior or information.
- *Statistics are not the whole answer:* Concentrating only on data can blind a manager to other relevant information. Silver's apt illustration: Two ballplayers have identical playing statistics. On off days, one volunteers at a soup kitchen, and the other snorts cocaine in nightclubs. "There is probably no way to quantify this distinction," writes Silver, "but you'd sure as hell want to take it into account."

HR professionals instinctively know that last point, but too often it leads to a view that performance management is more art than science. It's both art *and* science, and the key to using data is separating the signal (relevant but selective data) from the noise (irrelevant but plentiful data).

Two more observations about data come from Silver's *New York Times* colleague David Brooks: "First, [data are] really good at exposing when our intuitive view of reality is wrong. . . . Second, data can illuminate patterns of behavior we haven't yet noticed." Brooks, a skeptic concerning the rising popular notion that data analysis contains the answer to any question, concludes, "The data revolution is giving us wonderful ways to understand the present and the past. Will it transform our ability to predict and make decisions about the future?"[3]

Silver and Brooks remind devotees of data that information itself, in any quantity, is no substitute for wisdom. Data analysis is a brilliant tool leading HR forward to a higher-quality performance management system, and yet it is only part of the total system. Let's look at how raw information, data analysis, and wisdom can join to promote a better system—a system that not only measures performance, but also improves it and strengthens the company by making it more attuned to human needs and human promise.

The Meaning of Unexpected Signals

In traditional performance management you have perhaps two data points per person. One is a rating for performance, and the other is a rating for potential. Maybe the data points are on a 1-to-5 scale, and maybe there's some narrative, which is impossible to convert into data. By supplementing this with crowdsourced data, you go from one data point to dozens of data points. The single point of failure now is just part of a broader data set of performance judgments by the crowd.

Over time, these data also enable a regression analysis of the manager's ability to predict performance. This is an additional analysis tool, an unexpected signal in the noise. If the manager was giving somebody a 3, and the crowd gave the same person a 3, that's great. If he gives this person a 5 and the crowd gave a 5, that's great. But if the manager has a history of giving a dozen people a 2 when the crowd gives them a 4.5, now you've got a real discrepancy, and it's telling you more about the manager than it is about the employees. That's a reality check either way, using crowdsourced performance data about employees to evaluate the performance of the manager as a manager.

Now you can generate analytics from the data that uncover previously hidden signals. If an employee is rated 4.5 by the crowd and 2 by her manager, is she a flight risk? Should she be singled out for leadership training and succession planning? If you can start predicting management effectiveness and correlation with reality, you can start to predict dissonance between an employee and a manager.

Social recognition data are rich in nuanced information about what's really going on in the workplace. Ultimately, they're about placing people in the right position in the company and unlocking their potential.

Ultimately, the output of all of this is predicting the future about people. This is what crowdsourced data can give you because now you have a big enough data set. Compare this with the past, where you had one manager giving an employee a 4 out of 5. An abundance of data gives you much greater insight than one person picking a number could provide.

All this leaves HR with the task of selecting the right data, interpreting them in the right way, and adding the right nonquantifiable information to create a practice of more accurately predicting how certain employees will behave under certain conditions. In addition, HR must give managers incentive to overcome their unconscious biases that cause them to make judgments about employees using the wrong data or interpret data incorrectly. In the daily deluge of information about who is doing what, managers have to learn to distinguish the signal from the noise. Crowdsourced performance management through social recognition can help managers do this, but they will likely listen to the signal only if their own performance rating is on the line.

Using Data to Unlock Hidden Value

When it comes to identifying high-performing employees, traditional performance measures obviously matter. A sales representative has to hit the number, a product manager has to ship products, a logistics manager has to get the stuff to the right place on time. Business results give you that first cut—a global view of top performers.

Beyond those performance results, there are less easily quantified qualities that indicate high potential, and those qualities are found in social recognition data.

As you accumulate more data, a crowdsourced performance system renders more details about the social state of the workplace. At an advanced stage, these details help executives identify key groups within a workforce.

Here are several questions that help identify your top performers. Each question identifies a key metric that would otherwise be impos-

Why Untapped Potential Is Like an Endless Recession in Your Company

The crowd sees huge potential contribution and talent in Pete, but his manager doesn't tap that capability, so Pete isn't given the tools, training, and responsibility to achieve his true potential. One underappreciated employee might not be a disaster, but think of all the underutilized Petes in a 10,000-employee company, and you get an idea of the wasted capacity for higher performance.

This reminds me of a recession, in which the output capacity of an economy is depressed, so total wealth diminishes. When the economy eventually springs back into a growth phase, its latent capacity is utilized. It goes to maximum capacity, productivity is stretched, and wealth is created. More capacity is built, more people are hired, and the economy makes the most of its potential.

Underutilized talent and capability lying dormant in employees represent potential that is available almost for free. Uncover that potential with data, and you can use the latent potential of that 10,000-person company to generate a surge in performance.

In addition, when the data give details about employees' skill sets, management can see where they might be better used in the organization, making them more productive (and happier). Get the right people in the right seats, and the organization can achieve maximum output at minimum cost.

sible to identify objectively but that can be found by analyzing the social makeup of the workforce.

Who Are the Influencers?

It's hard to see who interacts with the broadest set of people. You can identify those with a psychological "fence" around themselves, or those whose jobs make it difficult to interact, but in a general office environment most interactions are informal. It's hard to know whom people talk to and whom they help. Looking at crowdsourced recognition data, you can map interactions outside of formal channels. Do recognition and thanks come from outside the department, the home office, or the home country? When you have a large set of inputs coming from a broad swath of the company, you can see who has a positive impact beyond their immediate colleagues.

A Bay-area tech company with a market-style bonus system (awarding stock options) awarded the third-largest bonus to a person with the ninth-largest paycheck—and that person was a remote developer, not even working in the office. She had been immensely helpful and influential among her remote colleagues. Letting the crowd recognize performance uncovers such hidden influence.[4]

Who Has Informal Power?

Informal power is held by people outside the hierarchy. They have big reputations, and they help others with their judgment and tacit knowledge. They are the thought leaders, the gurus of specific knowledge domains. They underpin a lot of the company's success without necessarily holding a title or position of formal power.

HR and managers need to know which employees have informal power and what it takes to keep them. Do they have what they need to be effective? Can a work or location change make the most of the positive power they accumulate as a matter of temperament? For example, are they part of a mentoring program? Are they formally rewarded for making connections with others?

Looking at social recognition data, you will uncover some people who have influence outside their normal sphere of work, department, or location. They propagate your cultural values in unexpected places and times.

The organization chart can't make a list of these people for you. Managers don't necessarily recognize their influence (especially managers outside their department, since influencers tend to go directly to the people they help, not "through channels"). Social recognition data can identify these people and the reasons they are influential. Once you have that knowledge, you can amplify their capacity by making it part of their job, part of their compensation, by giving them time or technology to make the most of the influence they already have.

Holders of informal power can be candidates for future leadership, along with the next category of hidden leaders.

Who Are Your Succession Candidates with Potential to Take Leadership Positions?

Succession candidates occupy a special niche in talent management. They're good at their jobs, and they also demonstrate the intangible qualities that make for great leaders. People look to them for direction and guidance. Those around them recognize their technical skill and also their ability to promote such necessary group qualities as teamwork, focus, and drive. They inspire confidence and make progress even in the face of ambiguity or partial information. They can differentiate between competitive advantage and busywork. They are good judges of people and performance. They form a pool of employees who will take over leadership as senior leaders move up or move on.

The earlier you can identify succession candidates, the more effectively you can direct their talents and knowledge toward management and leadership. Social recognition identifies them both in the amount of recognition they receive (especially from peers) and in the recognition they give (a key indicator of how they are tuned in to your social architecture).

Not everyone who promotes your culture is a succession candidate, however. There's another category of nonleadership temperaments that makes a positive impact—the cultural energizers.

Who Are the Cultural Energizers?

Cultural energizers are the keystones of the organization. They are the flag-bearers of your values; they naturally reinforce key behaviors and key beliefs across the workforce. They really believe in the mission, and they promote it to others at the next desk and around the world. (Some companies call them "cultural ambassadors.")

Say you're launching a social network for the company (like Chatter or Yammer). You want everyone to adopt the new technology, so you pay special attention to certain employees who are culturally influential. They get early training, they contribute to the implementation, and when they become enthusiastic about the social network, they naturally promote it. You leverage their cultural influencer to get everyone on board. This is about more than technology—it's about how the culture does business. The same is true for a safety project or a productivity or cost-cutting initiative: get the cultural energizers on board, and their influence will power the initiative throughout the organization.

You can use recognition data to identify the cultural energizers: They are consistently and clearly recognized for promoting specific values. The recognition they give is always connected to the larger values and causes of the company.

Cultural energizers are like influencers and those with informal power, with the difference being that they are focused on the organization's culture as much as they are on their work. I'm talking about exceptional believers, creators, and promoters of the company's culture day in and day out. There are only a few cultural influencers by definition, even in a well-aligned company. Since they are rare, you want to do what you can to identify them, promote them, and replicate their beliefs. They make great mentors, great spokespeople to customers and media, and great promoters, so you want to know who they are and hang onto them.

Who Is a Flight Risk?

A flight risk is an employee who you want to retain but, for some reason, is at risk of quitting. Recognition data indicate who a flight risk is by showing low recognition among high-performing or high-potential employees. They can show gaps between recognition from peers and from a manager. They can show that someone is giving a lot of recognition but receiving little—and the manager or HR executive should know why this is the case. These disconnects can signal trouble.

Is the employee unhappy or fearful? Is he or she insecure based on management oversight? Any time a high-potential employee, an influencer, or cultural energizer is flagged as a flight risk, it's not just worth investigating; it's worth jumping right into the situation and finding out the problem, because something has to change. In fact, the data predict that something *will* change unless the situation is fixed: Valuable people will quit.

What Are the Differences Among Locations?

As global organizations expand, they encounter new national cultures with different values and traditions from those the company adopted when it was smaller. Performance data can do little to illustrate these differences, especially because those data are culturally neutral—employees either hit the number or they don't.

(The same is subtly true among departments, by the way—you might have an aggressive sales culture and a cooperative customer care culture, all sitting in the same building and all supporting overall company values.)

Those who manage across cultures, whether geographical or psychological, have a hard time gathering data about who is influential or who is a flight risk. But social recognition data yield insight in two valuable ways: First, social recognition establishes "baseline" relationships between national or functional cultures. Public recognition among Asian, European, African, North American, and South American cultures can show subtle differences, for example, in how people recognize peers and how they recognize higher-ups.

Second, recognition activity over time creates data relationships of great value. If, for example, a department's recognition with respect to the value of "taking action together" declines, something's going on in that department. It might be good or bad, and recognition data won't tell the whole story, but they will trigger inquiry much earlier than other data, such as declining output, complaints, or people quitting. Remedies can be applied much sooner at much lower cost to the company.

The Benefits of Data Visualization

How can an executive extract meaning from all these data? This is one of the challenges of the big data revolution, and the answer lies in the growing movement toward data visualization.

Executive Insight

"It is better to use imprecise measures of what is wanted than precise measures of what is not."

—Russell Ackoff, Seminal Author and Educator
on Management Systems; Known as the
"Father of Operations Research"

Managers use a series of dashboards to compare and contrast data about recognition activity. An effective dashboard shows both data and relationships among data in a simple, visual representation—a visualization of data interacting with other data.

Figure 9.1 is a social recognition dashboard showing an HR executive how four of the groups mentioned above compare in recognition awards on a quarterly basis.

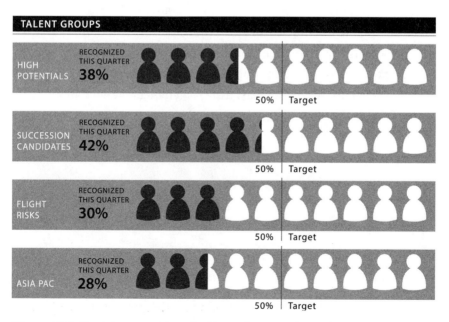

Figure 9.1 Social recognition dashboard comparing talent groups

Succession candidates are being well recognized, almost hitting the target number for this early-stage initiative. Flight risks are not being recognized as well, and aggregate recognition for the Asia Pacific division is lower still. Armed with this information, the executive can investigate. Is the program being promoted? Are succession candidates, the future leaders, achieving a high enough profile among their peers that their leadership talents are being groomed? Why or why not?

Historically, such quantitative insights were not captured at all, or if they were, the data and their insights were the property of a data analysis team. Data visualization drives these insights down to the manager level. Now a manager no longer needs to request information and interpretation from a data analysis team; it's available instantly, and in many forms based on the needs and goals of the manager, leader, or HR executive.

The manager's dashboard can also monitor how his or her performance judgment compares to that of the crowd, as shown in Figure 9.2.

This excerpt from a manager's dashboard compares who in her department is being recognized for great work with her own ratings. There are differences: High-Performing "5s" are overwhelmingly recognized by the crowd, but the people whose performance she's rated "4" aren't receiving as much attention from the crowd. Does she know why? Not yet, but this is a tipoff for her to ask herself some of the questions I've suggested above. At the least, this is a chance to check in with her HR executive to know if something should be done to bring the ratings into closer alignment.

REACH	12%	TARGET 10%	9%	TARGET 15%	45%	TARGET 35%	20%	TARGET 45%	79%	TARGET 55%
PERFORMANCE RATING	1		2		3		4		5	

Figure 9.2

Figure 9.3 shows a way to visualize the alignment of peer assessments through recognition and manager assessments through performance rating. The visual cues unearth vital clues about group alignment.

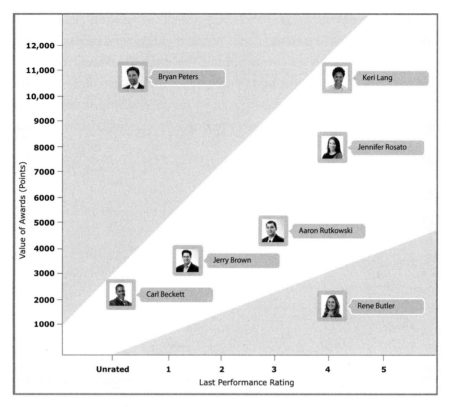

Figure 9.3 Comparing peer and manager assessments

The horizontal axis represents the manager's overall assessment of employees, using a traditional 1–5 system. The vertical axis quantifies the value of recognition awards individuals have received.

At the upper right, Keri Lang is rated a top performer by both her manager and the crowd. At the upper left, by contrast, Bryan Peters is highly regarded by the crowd but rated as a poor performer by his manager. Again, this begs the question, "Why such a misalignment?" Carl Beckett, in the lower left, hasn't been recognized much, but also is not rated by his manager—the explanation is simple: Carl's been on the job for only a few weeks.

Outliers appear in the shaded areas in this visualization's upper left and lower right. The neutral zone between these areas (dubbed the "hurricane zone" after weather map conventions) contains those employees whose assessment by the manager and the crowd are aligned.

This type of visualization and many others can be tweaked, adjusted, and created according to the needs of the organization, its culture, and its goals. Data visualization simplifies the analysis of large data sets and gives the line manager basic predictive and interpretive tools. What was once invisible and frustrating is now visible and ready to use. What was never sought because it was impossible to find is now obvious.

Crowdsourcing the Rest of HR

For a moment, think of what crowdsourcing can do for HR's other domains:

Recruitment

Social media have emerged as the next big thing in recruitment. HR and recruiters look online for candidates at broad networking services like LinkedIn and also at niche sites like MediaBistro.com. Employee referral programs have proven that it's possible to enlist the crowd to find recruits who are a good fit for culture, skills, diversity, values—all kinds of qualities—and this is essentially extending the company's reach through employee social networks.

Managing recruitment goes beyond sourcing candidates, and a growth area for HR will be managing a company's reputation within the universe of social media. It's happening now with Facebook pages that get the crowd of employees to tell a company's story, promote its values, and attract talent.

Workplace Wellness Programs

Weight Watchers has proved for generations that social support helps people make positive changes in their health habits. Social media platforms connect employees who are losing weight, controlling high blood pressure, exercising, quitting smoking, and providing support for a hundred other life situations. This is essentially the same as social recognition. For HR, crowdsourcing platforms can provide rich data on participation and achievement; for example, if the Indianapolis office is very successful in its wellness programs, HR can actually visualize the networks, individuals, and activities that drive that success, and duplicate it in other offices.

Health

Closely related to wellness are health insurance programs and health initiatives. The bigger the company, the more likely it is to self-insure, bypassing health insurance companies. When you have 20,000 employees, it's cost-effective to do this, spreading insurance risk across a broad population as insurance companies do. With self-insurance, a company has a potential gold mine of health and wellness information that can be used (with privacy protections in place) to cut the cost of healthcare for all. And the ways in which the crowd uses healthcare services can guide the company to provide the most needed services to the right people at the right time. If smokers quit at a higher rate than the national average or if every overweight person drops ten pounds and keeps it off, you'll have a healthier workforce. And you'll save a lot of money. The mechanisms and crowd psychology are closely linked to social recognition. For example, on social media platforms smokers share experiences and tips on everything from nicotine gum to harnessing the power of habit to break unhealthy habits. Taking that a step further into the social recognition realm, support groups can track who's gone the longest without tobacco, who cut back the fastest, who is giving the most encouragement to others and celebrating each others' progress.

Ten years ago "wellness" meant a poster in the break room. Now it can mean harnessing the power of crowds to create all kinds of value for the company. The same applies to initiatives in safety, for example.

(continued)

> **Mobile Applications**
> Cloud-based computing means that all these HR activities can take place anywhere, anytime, because they can be made into mobile applications. That's a benefit for lifestyle programs because it means the value is no longer dependent on someone sitting at a desk from 9 to 5. Wellness, health, recruiting—these activities should take place outside the workplace and the workday. With smartphones and an engaged workforce, they do. And that benefits everyone.

A Compensation Revolution

The information technology research firm Gartner published an extraordinary report titled *2012 Strategic Road Map for Employee Performance Management*. The study confirmed the shortcomings of traditional performance reviews and pay-for-performance plans reviewed earlier in this book. It recommended a social recognition program as a solution.

Gartner then went on to propose an even more advanced form of crowdsourced performance management. Going forward, it proposed that companies should measure, adjust, and balance their investment in forms of compensation annually. "The business needs and macroeconomic environment will change," it asserted, and so compensation itself must become more flexible and more aligned with the total input of managers' judgment and social recognition data.

Gartner is saying, "Take a percentage of your total rewards and drive it through the company as small, incremental awards that are crowdsourced from the company's employees." Review it every year to see if it is effective, and alter the ratio of how much of that total rewards budget you're putting through is socially generated pay. Let behavior and results determine whether social recognition is adding value to a compensation system.

It takes effort for Fortune 500 companies to do something like that. It's not like just installing an enterprise social network like Chatter. Rearchitecting how you pay 20,000 employees must pass a high standard of value for a company like Gartner to recommend such an undertaking.

At IGN Entertainment, a division of News Corporation, they call it "viral pay."[5] At Symantec, Intuit, IHG, and others they have different names for crowdsourced rewards, but it all follows Gartner's recommendation. Incremental payments in the form of social recognition awards are leading a revolution in compensation. In the days and years to come, the best employees will surface in unexpected places and in unexpected ways because an enabling technology has rendered the invisible plain. Pay for performance will become more accurate, democratic, and targeted. And employees who make the greater contributions will receive the greater rewards.

10   A Vision for 2020

Liz, now the global vice president of product strategy at Hydro-lab, studied her personnel budget for 2021 with Rebecca. The projected budget and performance expectations were based on seven years of crowdsourced data. The social dashboard for Dana's 52-person department, with employees on three continents, rendered 3-D models on a world map as the two executives changed scenarios. Each country's data sources contained a host of crowdsourced information for her planning:

- *Compensation: 50 percent fixed and 50 percent variable*
- *Benefits: 24 percent above compensation, configurable with 8 variable programs*
- *Performance measures averaging 20 variables, adjustable by subgroup and country*
- *Recognition values*
  - *Safe employees and safe customers*

> ■ *Show focus and determination.*
>
> ■ *Demonstrate integrity daily.*
>
> ■ *Nurture engagement, energy and enthusiasm.*
>
> ■ *Unite in execution.*
>
> *Rebecca said, "Trevor will announce the sixth recognition value at the global management meeting next week."*
>
> *"It's official now?" Liz asked.*
>
> *"Only the senior managers know, but you can add it to your system now. Just wait until the announcement to discuss it with your group."*
>
> *Liz created a new values category in her system, and typed:*
> **Build a Positivity Dominated Workplace.**

What would an ideal performance management system accomplish? What benefits might it bring to executives, HR, managers, and employees at large in the coming years?

An ideal system will combine the best components of a traditional review with social recognition. It will be self-adjusting, with data analysis to design the right mix of rewards for each individual, always encouraging people to improve performance across a spectrum of tasks and outcomes. It will provide constant feedback to both individuals and their managers, while informing the community at large of progress. It will harness the wisdom of crowds to give accurate and specific feedback on individual performance, and it will harness the power of data analysis to connect performance to profits.

More than anything, it will continuously drive company behavior toward a deliberate, strategic culture. It will be positive and self-monitoring and empower managers to manage better while encouraging self-management at all levels.

The conversation today in the HR community is moving toward that vision for 2020. Pay will be reconfigured to influence and promote crowdsourced performance management. Once-hidden data on employee engagement will be at managers' fingertips, and executives will leverage the resulting social graph of their companies to drive culture.

Here is how this vision improves work and life for everyone.

Employees: Crowdsourcing Compensation

There's a mainstream system of performance evaluation today in which the crowd determines an employee's pay. Those workplaces are called restaurants.

Consider restaurant servers who earn a huge part of their pay through tips. This is engrained in U.S. culture because we're trying to produce better experiences in a restaurant (in addition to the food). So we incentivize them to curry favor with the diners, deliver great service, have a positive attitude, and basically take care of the customers. They get paid more by the appreciative consumers of those actions—the customers.

As you go up the restaurant value chain, to fancier and more expensive restaurants, tips (which you might think of as crowdsourced pay) become bigger as a percentage of total pay. The server in a diner might take home $50 a day for excellent service, and the server in a three-star restaurant might take home $500 for the same number of meals served— even though their official salaries (typically low) aren't very far apart.

Jobs in premier restaurants are highly desired, and restaurant owners reward the best servers with the best tables and the best shifts. The customers likewise reward great service. Unconsciously, they've established a pretty good performance management system. (In many good restaurants, even busboys and other near-invisible staff members get a share of the tips because they contribute to the experience. The wine glasses and silverware are spotless because the person who washes the dishes does a great job.)

What if, in addition to customers tipping, the hostess were to tip the waitresses, and the waitresses were to tip the hostesses and the cooks and the busboys, all drawing from a pool of money like a recognition bonus program? You'd have more than just the positive mental energy coming from the waitress to the customer; you'd also have it between the waitress and the hostess because they're looking for it. They're acting in ways to get it, and they're encouraging each other.

Apply that to an office environment: Say that somebody comes into the company with a salary of $40,000. Perhaps he begins with a base guarantee of $30,000 with the expectation that he'll receive around $10,000 in small, incremental awards in a recognition program, a 75/25 percent allocation of salary and bonus. It's a crowdsourced bonus, coming from the wider community, and he's going to get it in increments averaging $100. That's a lot of awards.

Now let's get out of the conceptual comfort zone with a thought experiment: What if the split were 50/50? Now recognition awards are outside the realm of "bonus" and are part of the regular pay package, but a variable figure. What would that create in terms of the atmosphere, the cultural temperature, and the morale in that company? Everybody would be helping everybody because that's how they get most of their reward, and it's self-perpetuating because it becomes a much more enjoyable place to work. Everybody is happier, so performance improves.

Such employees will net the same amount of money from the company, but their attitude must fundamentally change. In order to accumulate awards, they will continuously find opportunities to help others, to improve performance, and to feed the narrative of continuous improvement. Their personalities and the way they interact with people improve. They meet and greet people in a more energetic and positive way. They're earning $100 bonuses through their daily behaviors and actions, and they're going to be helping everybody. Because they have the power to reward others, they help to weave a stronger social fabric in the company. As they nominate others for awards, they will become more conscious of company goals, values, and teamwork. And they won't take these things for granted—they'll be active builders of culture.

Managers: Finally, a Real Performance Narrative

In the future, with the right software, managers will monitor the performance of their teams in a constant narrative of positive events, com-

> ## Rating Performance in the Professions
>
> Crowdsourced reward is coming to once-sacred business arrangements. As The Affordable Care Act ties some healthcare payments to patient outcomes and cost containment, hospitals are exploring proposals to have patient feedback factored into the pay of doctors.[1] University professors are exploring ways to rate their popularity in massive open online courses (MOOCs), because when there's income to be made from online education, the most popular professors hope to benefit from high ratings from the crowd of users.
>
> What's next? By 2020, will lawyers, accountants, and the clergy receive some of their pay in small, incremental recognition awards?

paring these to measures such as deadlines, quality control, and quotas. When performance review time comes around, they'll have a full narrative of what employees did, how they did it, the impact of their actions, and the results.

They'll see deeper into the social matrix that enables work to be done faster, more creatively, and more efficiently. Social recognition input from the crowd will create a story around each employee based on subjective experiences that amount to an objective measure of each employee's impact. Software will compare that social impact with bottom-line performance data to reveal subtle patterns of behavior, communication, and action that amount to best practices but that could hardly have been detected earlier.

In this data-rich environment, relationships will become more transparent and more important than ever. Employees who are temperamentally quiet but helpful will be noticed and rewarded without having to boast or maneuver for attention.

The long-term effects of small actions will be documented. Old wisdom about the magnifying effect of small acts of insight, creativity, and support over time will be affirmed. Because recognition can actually record the small events that lead to big initiatives in real time, everyone will learn the value of certain practices.

At performance review time, managers and every member of their teams will have a host of stories and data to shape the conversation. No longer a painful process of checking boxes on a form, performance management will be a lively dialogue based on real-world relationships, events, and behaviors.

It's more than just congratulations, because now the different strengths of the staff members—not just their talents or temperaments—become apparent in their behaviors. Now when giving Petra her performance review, manager Charlie can discuss all the times she's won awards, all the times people have congratulated her on those awards, what people have said, and where the awards have come from. The software will quantify the value of Petra's extra effort and tie it directly to goals met and profits made.

Social recognition will help individuals improve performance because public celebration of successful effort teaches everyone what works. The crowd will become a coach of best practices.

Combined with the discipline of the traditional performance reviews—for compliance as well as structured feedback—the social recognition performance review has created a climate of continuous improvement in Charlie's department.

Executives: A Complete Social Narrative of Performance

The next few years will be most exciting for executives. Thanks to the merging of traditional review and social recognition, senior executives can finally read the invisible but ultrapowerful performance social narrative of the company. Who is inspiring great work? Who is engaged, loyal, and energetic? Who is reaching out across "silos"? Which managers are helping their staff improve performance in specific, measurable steps? How is compensation directly related to behaviors that result in profits and "living the mission"?

Executives will be able to generate lists of employees with informal power, and they will know who is influential. They will fast-track succession plans based on social recognition data, and upward mobility will have less friction. Thanks to social recognition and the data it produces, HR and business leaders can finally be proactive rather than reactive. They have real numbers across a whole spectrum of behaviors that can be adjusted, managed, and changed as needed. They have a rapid response system to alert all employees to changes in business priorities *and* a rapid reporting system to show where employees are quick to change. Leaders and their managers now have a performance management system that actually manages performance in the context of a community, with all the thousands or hundreds of thousands of daily interactions that characterize a modern company, organization, or community. And finally, everyone in the company has a personal stake in managing performance. That level of engagement might well be the greatest cultural benefit of a new performance management paradigm.

And in this new world, executives will have what they always dreamed of: A meaningful percentage of total pay will be paid to top performers based on their positive influence on the crowd. To find these top performers, they need only "follow the money!"

HR: The Rise of Reputation Capital

Human resources is going to face a fascinating dilemma in the coming decade: whether to cede control of employees' reputations to public view. Should an outstanding employee, who receives a lot of recognition and awards, be able to release that information to public view?

It's a conundrum like the one we've seen since the web made everyone's résumé available—HR recruiters love the access to talent provided by résumé databases and networking services, but HR managers don't love the fact that their best people cannot be kept under wraps and are the target of poaching by other HR people. Some of the world's best companies try hard to obscure the identities of their rising stars so that their competitors won't tempt those stars to leave.

Face it: Reputation has been the currency of recruiting for a long time. HR recruiters search databases for candidates who attended prestigious universities, worked at top companies, and won awards. Achievements are the narrative of many job interviews. Social recognition awards are just a new form of these. One way or another, it will become part of an employee's profile.

The real dilemma will turn on transparency. How might an internal social recognition system become public? It is private information, highly valuable to a company. Should a recognition count go on an employee's LinkedIn profile?

I think that this crosses the line into private company information, but workarounds will appear because while the system belongs to the company, the reputation belongs to the employee. It will be an evolutionary process. At first employees will simply mention their recognition awards as part of their job narrative; later they might quantify the distinction by saying, "Fifty percent of my pay came from discretionary recognition awards from my peers and managers."

Even if a person's recognition awards become public, the great value of a recognition system is its power to map the total social architecture of a team, a department, or a company. While bits of raw data will inevitably become public, the data analysis—finding the valuable patterns in all the human interactions of a workplace—will remain firmly in the hands of the company.

HR will have to acknowledge that most information that can be legally made public will in fact be made public. Instead of chasing after employees to hide their light under a bushel, HR and company leadership should focus on creating a Positivity Dominated Workplace and a culture so powerful, so appreciative, and so energized that employees feel an ever-stronger connection with the company.

There will always be reasons good employees leave that are beyond the control of any executive. People move, look for different challenges, change, and grow. Businesses likewise move, grow, and adapt to a changing world. Rather than trying in vain to prevent employees from leaving,

HR leaders should be busy building the reputation capital of the company, branding that company as the place outstanding people want to work.

Reputation capital by 2020 will serve HR in ways beyond recruiting. As more and more data accumulate, managers will be able to assemble virtual teams with complementary strengths. Employees will understand each other's ways of working. Trust, communication, and cooperation will bloom along with an ever-greater understanding of how diverse groups come together to achieve ever-greater results.

Lifelogging the Organization

What if a social recognition system had existed in the early days at IBM or GE? At Apple or Microsoft? What could you learn from the social narrative of the beginnings of these companies?

A little while ago, a person who had been with my company for seven years moved away. I looked her up on our recognition platform, and I saw this amazing array of interactions between her and other people, all detailed in awards that she'd won over the years. I was able to see her influence on all of the company, her influence and involvement in myriad projects—a huge number of her successes and achievements, a lot of the company's successes and achievements, and the social relationships that existed there and evolved over time. I was able to see projects I had completely forgotten about from years ago. I could see little projects that bloomed into great new products and things that we thought were a big deal that turned out to be not so important. But then, that's the history of companies. All these small projects add up to a company.

Then I thought about previous jobs I had worked in. I worked in three companies after college before I arrived where I am now. I worked in each of them for a year and a half or two years, but there's no record of what I did in those companies and no way of finding out. There's no way of going back and saying, "What projects did I work on? Whom did I know? How did I interact with people?" There's no way to know. Think of the insights not gained, because they were not recorded.

In 2020, the lifelogging feature of social recognition will emerge as a valuable company asset. Great companies have known this for a long time, which is why they preserve a historical narrative. When you go into the head offices of Hewlett-Packard or Intel in California, you'll see that their lobbies have been turned into museums. At HP, a company that has changed and changed again through the years, there are still pictures of the old garage where Bill Hewitt and Dave Packard started. There are timelines that are projected on the walls about all the successes and changes. At the executive offices of Citi in New York there are glass cases with mementos like an old stock ticker machine from 100 years ago.

Companies value their history and they should; they're people, behaving every day and writing their own history. We value national cultures and study the records of history to learn more about ourselves, who we are, and where we might go.

With everyone recognizing every aspect of performance in the social network that is a company, it's possible to start writing that history of who we are. And that's the starting point for imagining where we might go.

APPENDIX: IMPLEMENTING SOCIAL RECOGNITION

In the experience of our customers, successful social recognition programs share several operating principles. Like any management initiative, social recognition needs careful planning and implementation in order to produce a healthy return on investment. The following principles allow organizations to customize their programs and prevent the managerial and psychological "disconnects" that plague less effective programs.

Executive Sponsorship, Defined Goals, and Frequent Communication

Support from senior management is critical to success in any initiative, and this is especially true in managing corporate culture. In market-leading companies, strategic initiatives are managed using process, metrics, incentives, and accountability, and senior executives monitor these. Success requires a rigorous methodology such as Six-Sigma's DMAIC (Define, Measure, Analyze, Improve, Control) and meaningful measurement. Managers must be held accountable for goals, including percentage of employees awarded, employee satisfaction and engagement scores, the match of award distribution to the bell curve, and the frequency of awards. Sponsorship and communication of the recognition program cannot be left to human resources staff members; it must come from a group of unified top leaders—all of them.

The more exactly you can plan such details as award levels, the more precise your measurements of award activity and money spent will be. With a defined goal of 80 to 90 percent participation in the recognition program, your data will be actionable. With defined participation goals for division heads and managers, the cultural management of recognition can take hold.

Whatever your goals, they must be written down. As in any business planning process, supporting your strategic goals will be specific program goals and objectives. Here's an example from Intuit:

Intuit's Recognition Ambition

Drive higher employee engagement at Intuit.

Improve employee satisfaction survey results.

Create a culture of recognition throughout Intuit.

Continue to make Intuit a "Best Place to Work."

Each of these goals can be affirmed over time—does employee engagement improve? (You can measure engagement objectively by such standards as the Gallup Q12 or Towers Watson models.) What do employee satisfaction surveys tell over time? Are line managers able over time to observe and describe changes in both commitment and alignment?

Ambitions may be stated as strategic goals for the recognition program, as in this example from Symantec:

Strategic Goals for Recognition at Symantec

- All recognition programs globally will be migrated to one platform, with one common brand and one executive dashboard.
- One global strategic recognition solution.
- Drive employee loyalty.
- Reward behaviors that support company values.
- Local impact and relevance for all employees GLOBALLY.

These are some of the most popular goals; yours must be specific to your organization's ambitions, market position, and challenges. Take time to define these goals clearly, for without them, recognition will not be taken seriously as a strategic initiative. (Without clear goals, moreover, you'll be tempted to judge your program's effectiveness by anecdotes or gut feel. This almost guarantees program mediocrity.)

Executive sponsorship includes frequent communication about the program. Our experience shows that a successful launch happens when managers have seven to eight opportunities to see messages about the program in a short period of time and in various media (online, in voice mail from the CEO, in e-mail, in training, from peers, and in hands-on practice). We've also seen that 85 percent of successful recognition programs touch employees every two weeks in a variety of ways, including testimonials, success stories, training brushups, employee endorsements, and visual communication like posters and short video messages.

Establish a Single, Clear, Global Strategy

Global means universal and applies whether you work for a small organization or a multinational giant. A clear global strategy requires a clear outcome. Some examples of the outcomes that might be sought are increased customer satisfaction, increased employee engagement scores, more repeat business, higher net promoter scores, increased product quality, or reduced costs.

Many clients have come to us with multiple, scattered, and even conflicting recognition programs, which lead to divisions within the company, confusion, and wasted money. A global strategy creates a single recognition brand and vocabulary. It creates clear visibility into budgets and can be audited. Executives in different divisions, locations, and markets can view uniform metrics that provide insight into program adoption, operation, and results.

You have to treat all employees equally. We have an expression across global companies, *parity of esteem*, which means that whether employees are in Ireland, Poland, Japan, or Argentina, they are all treated with the same regard.

Equal treatment does not mean identical treatment, however. A clear global strategy includes recognizing the differences in languages and local cultures and assigning award values to align with the local standard of living. Rewards must be personally meaningful, culturally relevant, and equitable in the number of options and value of rewards from country to country.

If a company already has ad hoc recognition programs in place, the transition to a single strategy will be challenging. Some programs will have to be cancelled, and some people will be very attached to their ideas of recognition. To ensure consistency as well as being able to manage the program, you have to integrate a single technology platform. You have to establish a return on investment in new technology across divisions (and factor in the savings of cancelling the ad hoc programs and consolidating everyone on one platform).

Frame the Goals of a Social Recognition Practice Early

Framing your program ambitions in detail informs program design. Recognition takes place in day-to-day management. Unlike payroll or tax reporting, for example, a recognition system is not a matter of installing a new software package. Hard-to-measure factors, such as the adaptability of your line managers, can play a significant role in the effectiveness of recognition. Early in your design of a recognition program, ask the questions that set a size and scope for your efforts, such as:

- How aggressive do we want to be? (For example: How soon do we hit goal A? How soon do we hit goal B?)
- What resources do we need to start and continue the program?
- How fast can our managers learn this new skill?
- What other programs are in the pipeline at this time?
- Which departments (e.g., training, communications, finance) need to be involved in ongoing operation of the program?

- How do we report progress?
- What is the best rollout path?

Answering these questions in detail early on results in a more cost-effective and powerful program later.

Once you have clear goals, translate those ambitions into measurable achievements to make recognition meaningful to executive leadership. Recognition metrics should:

1. Reflect what's important in the corporate culture based on the company's values.
2. Measure significance relative to your strategic goals, such as changes in productivity, cost, and retention.
3. Show how certain recognition behaviors drive employee performance (which also identifies best practices within your culture).
4. Link recognition to the organization's financial statements and corporate goals.

Examples of strong strategic metrics include:

- More than 90 percent of employees are touched by the program (as nominators or recipients).
- One-year survey confirms that 90 percent of employees agree that "the program helps motivate sustained high performance."
- Program reaches all geographic and demographic groups of the organization.
- Award distribution matches performance bell curve.
- Within six months of training, managers' units have reached target award frequency.
- Six-month survey shows 90 percent of managers participating.
- One unified system meets budgetary goals at six- and twelve-month milestones.
- Two-year survey shows double-digit increase in employee satisfaction.

- Two-year survey shows double-digit increase in employees qualified as engaged.
- Company values selected as award reasons by department, division, and/or region, as appropriate.

Measurement means relevance. Without it, any project tends to justify itself. The lonely corners of companies are cluttered with once-promising initiatives that lack measured success or failure. Often in recognition, standards of success are applied later in the game, simply to legitimize the project instead of at the outset; this makes the metrics irrelevant.

The bottom line is this: If you don't know what you're working toward before you begin, how will you know when you've achieved what you're supposed to achieve?

Determine your metrics *before* execution begins, and then faithfully report against those metrics on a regular schedule, even if the outcome isn't what you hoped for. Negative results can be the most valuable because they show you the areas where you most need to improve. In companies where such failure is permitted, continual improvement is possible, not just in a recognition program but across the board.

If your organization has project managers, use their tools (or better yet, get a project manager on the recognition team) to keep the setup and execution on schedule for a smooth program launch. Then use periodic surveys to measure such factors as:

- Employee and manager participation
- Number and/or percentage of awards given
- Size of awards given
- Program budget
- Impact on employee morale
- Impact on customer satisfaction
- Impact on productivity
- Follow-up actions taken (if the program reveals management or employee problems)
- Impact on employee attraction, retention, and turnover
- Impact on engagement

Identify recognition opportunities as you implement the program. Recognize managers who understand and embrace the program, who see improvements in their staff as the program continues, and who encourage and teach recognition as mentors to other managers. In other words, make progress in recognition important enough to recognize and reward!

Align Social Recognition with Company Values and Strategic Objectives

When individual-recognition moments are consciously linked to company values and goals, employees understand how their actions directly affect the culture. They see how their behavior fits into the big picture. They gain both a sense of efficacy and a sense of accountability within the big picture.

For all this to work, you need to track the program in a far more rigorous and disciplined way than the usual recognition effort attempts. If you can count the number of times in a company that somebody thanks somebody else for going the extra mile on a value like quality, this can give you an indication of the amount of discretionary effort that's being expended in and around quality. Management science suggests that you then add that all up and you accumulate this information. You put it together graphically in a histogram, and you compare a quarter with a quarter, a country with a country, a division with a division. This can give you enormous insight into how your values are turning into behaviors and are displayed in discretionary effort across the company.

Monthly dashboards illustrate for managers the traction of each value, whether by region, division, or department. Targeted management intervention in places where values are ignored or misunderstood then becomes possible. The dashboards represent people's behavior, which as we've said is the reality check of a company's culture.

Create an Opportunity for All to Participate

When only a few elite members of the organization receive infrequent, high-value awards, it is impossible to affect the broader corporate culture. Giving many lower-value rewards to employees across the company, by contrast, creates a stronger impact on the company. Every recognition moment doubles as a marketing and communication moment, reinforcing company values in a positive employment experience. As more employees participate, the company gains greater voluntary alignment with shared values. As more participate, the social recognition data gathered become richer, more detailed, and more accurately reflective of the entire company's attachment to particular values. As a side benefit, the presence of a broad-based recognition practice breaks down psychological barriers of class and rank, thus decreasing the chance of employee alienation from management.

Authenticity is golden. In the age of the Internet, when employees anonymously share information about the inner workings and culture of a company, the truth will come out. When a company's leadership effectively rewards and recognizes corporate values, the company will be celebrated in cyberspace by its own employees. On Facebook, on Twitter, on LinkedIn, in e-mail, and on job message boards, employees will confirm the company's legitimacy to each other and to the world. That kind of advertising can't be bought. However, if comments are negative, that kind of criticism can't be countered with a press release about company values. In sustaining a culture, you have to walk the talk.

High participation levels get employees involved in promoting the cultural change among each other. Think of how eBay users have the star ratings for buyers and sellers, to regulate each other for trustworthiness and customer service. The CEO of eBay doesn't decide whether a vendor is supporting the values of honesty, service, and transparency—the users do. In the same way, wide participation and peer-to-peer interactions through the recognition program support the values promoted by recognition. Exceptional employees are recognized by the group, and the group looks to them for informal guidance. Executive management needs only to structure the recognition program so that it reflects critical values (or a big global initiative), and the recognition program will provide incentive for behavior that supports it.

Harness the Power of Individual Choice

The relevance of an award to an individual is more important than its material value, especially in a global program. When developing the roster of awards available, managers must consider the demographics of a worldwide workforce that might span four generations, all with different expectations and driving forces. Locally based choice ensures that the award will always be culturally appropriate and to the recipient's taste while avoiding the varying cultural norms that simply cannot be known by every manager everywhere in the world. Allowing people to choose what is meaningful and personal to them increases the significance of the award. (Movie tickets aren't motivating for someone who doesn't like movies. A cupcake won't motivate someone on a diet. A designated parking space means nothing to someone who rides the bus.) Noncash rewards in the form of gift cards to local high-value venues take rewards beyond compensation to a socially acceptable trophy status everywhere in the world.

Individual choice of rewards also aligns well with the expectations of younger talent, the future leaders of your organization. They are savvy about media and brands, not shy about expressing preferences, and conditioned by technology and temperament to express their preferences.

Include Recognition in a System of Total Rewards

Executives new to recognition often ask, "Can't we just give bonuses?"

Giving cash rewards for good performance is a severely limiting form of recognition and motivation. To make the point, we call on the total rewards model as described by management consultancy WorldatWork, whose recognition practice leader Alison Avalos told us the following:

> Compensation is the must in the package, but in the end rewards are not only about pay. Recognition can be used to meet specific

needs to differentiate one company from the next. Recognition is customizable, informal, and easy to shift based on what you're trying to accomplish. Most high-performance companies have figured this out. What works today might not work in five years; typically a workforce is going to evolve. Today, flexibility is at the center of the map.

A total rewards system includes compensation, benefits, work-life factors, performance and recognition, and development and career opportunities. It includes both tangible income and intangible rewards. The goal of total rewards is to achieve the highest return on investment with the optimal mix of rewards. In practice, managers calibrate and apply this menu of rewards to attract, motivate, engage, and retain employees individually. This leads directly to improved performance and business results.

Recognition caters to the psychic investment you make in yourself and others make in you. That individual focus has to carry through in an award that crystallizes the message. Recognition is often forgotten, however, by staff members at all levels who typically see only pay, benefits, and sometimes equity in the company reflected in their compensation statements. This is a problem of visibility, not value.

In *Reward Systems: Does Yours Measure Up?*,[1] human resources pioneer Steve Kerr observes that compensation, benefits, and incentives have an easy-to-measure cash value. He goes on to describe what he calls *prestige awards* when, for example, an employee becomes a member of the prestigious President's Club or gets the window office. Kerr also describes a category of awards he calls *content rewards*, which entail feedback, conversations between managers, and recognition, either one to one or publicly demonstrated. These content rewards are a continuous performance lever to reinforce the culture at an everyday level. (Other content rewards can include giving an employee a new role, exposing him to training, or nominating her to an important committee.)

A social recognition program is paid for in cash, but its accretive value, memorable human connections, and built-in flexibility make it more adaptable to the goal of supporting values. In a well-designed program, recognition is more abundant than cash because, typically, a recognition award has an average value of $100, whereas a base salary might be $60,000. Or a bonus might be $5,000. So that $100 is obviously much less scarce than a $5,000 bonus.

This begs the question: Should we think of recognition as fundamentally a cost outlay, like the cost of employee health insurance, or an investment in the quality of management? Companies that have made a success of recognition see it as part of the "total rewards" view of compensation because it helps management succeed and optimizes performance, delivering an impressive return on investment.[2]

Cash Versus Noncash Rewards

Ask employees if they want cash or some other reward, and they will nearly always say cash, believing it gives them ultimate flexibility. Cash rewards might not benefit the organization, however. If your investment in recognition is nothing but cash prizes, you're making an investment that gives you the worst possible return for your investment. To understand why, let's look at where that cash goes:

Let's say you receive $100 cash in a spot recognition program. How would you use that award in your personal life? It would probably be distributed in your paycheck as just a line item on your paystub and then deposited into your household checking account. Income taxes are taken out of the award amount, so it gets reduced to about $75.

An employee making $50,000 a year receives a biweekly before-tax paycheck of $1,923.07 and an after-tax (at a 25 percent tax rate) deposit of about $1,442.31. Does a one-time change in an employee's pay from $1,442.31 to $1,517.31, two weeks after the recognition moment, seem memorable? We doubt anyone would notice.

Studies with our clients show that for those using cash awards in their recognition program, many (and sometimes most) of the employees who receive cash awards have no recollection of how they used those awards.

Why is this? Because cash is slippery. Welcome as it might have been, the emotional payoff was fleeting, and the award was undistinguishable from other compensation. In Maslow's hierarchy, many cash awards end up going to pay for life's necessities—the lowest tier of Maslow's pyramid.

Now let's look at what happens with a noncash reward: You receive a $100 gift certificate in a spot recognition program that allows you to choose how and when you want to redeem the certificate. How would you use that in your personal life? First of all, you would likely have to take some time to decide how to use the certificate, already making this reward more memorable than the cash award described above. In this instance, the award remains separate from your paycheck and gives you more discretionary purchasing power. You can choose the award's emotional content. You might make an impulse purchase without guilt. You might buy a special gift for a friend. You might give the certificate to a charity important to you. Every one of these decision points prolongs the psychic payoff. And at every point in the decision process you remember, "I got this because I demonstrated innovation in meeting that deadline."

Study after study shows that *noncash rewards* are the key to improved performance. These rewards are cost-effective as well. They are more flexible, affordable, and immediate than salary. Paid in the "currency" of recognition, these rewards can be intangible (initially) but no less real than material income.

Katie Scott, director of global compensation at LSI, remembers the moment senior executives realized the relative weakness of cash awards. She was advocating a change from cash to gift cards in a meeting and this timely conversation occurred: "Our controller was in the room and our SVP had just given her one of these $200 awards. It had been delivered in cash and just plopped into her paycheck. And he said to her, 'What did you do with that award that I gave you?' She said, 'I didn't even realize it was in my paycheck.' It was a perfect story in the room about why our existing recognition [program] wasn't working, and why cash wasn't necessarily king."

Include Recognition Activity in MBO Targets

Business measures activity for understanding and control: "If you can measure it, you can manage it." Measurement is a reality check. If your recognition program is to achieve that level of strategic cultural management, you have to monitor its activity day to day.

Research Insight

Tangible and Intangible Rewards

"The traditional forms of motivation are compensation and benefits. The problem with these tangible rewards is that they are short-term motivators. The more people get, the more they develop an entitlement mindset. Adding more and more tangible rewards does not necessarily increase motivation or engagement. However, taking away tangible benefits or entitlements really de-motivates or disengages people.

"On the other hand, intangible rewards, such as a 'thank you,' 'good job,' or effective coaching, let people know their managers care about them and value their contributions. The more intangible forms of motivation the better—they raise engagement levels by helping people feel connected.

"The additional advantage of using intangible rewards is that while offering them greatly increases levels of engagement and motivation, withholding them tends not to have a significant long-term de-motivating impact. Additionally, intangible forms of motivation are not costly to provide. So for a small investment of time in showing appreciation, the resulting improvement in engagement and connectivity can be huge. The key is in giving credible, sincere, and respectful appreciation."[3]

—From "Human Potential Untangled,"
by Kevin J. Sensenig

To manage the success of a recognition program, you need to measure the act of recognition itself. This can be done by giving your managers targets and having part of their management by objectives (MBO) bonuses depend on hitting those targets. For example, "You have to give ten awards to your team this quarter. It's in your objectives. And I'm going to measure that."

In practice, most acts by employees that are to be recognized are not things that are formally measured against preset goals. These acts are spontaneous and depend on the employee's good judgment. They are inspired from within. They are a surprise.

Here's an example: Globoforce office manager Kim organized a day-long off-site meeting. She did a fabulous job. Nobody sat down with Kim beforehand and said, "If you organize the off-site by 5 p.m. on Friday, and we all get our meals on time, and you go the extra mile to make it a success, then you're going to get an award." That would be an incentive. Instead, Kim made a series of decisions on her own that ensured that the meeting ran smoothly and was successful. That's the kind of behavior that should be recognized (and we did recognize it).

With incentives, managers are encouraged to reward what's measured; with recognition, they are encouraged to reward subjectively and spontaneously.

Is it contrary to the spirit of recognition to place a certain number of recognition moments in an MBO plan? Doesn't that make acting on recognition an incentive? Leaving aside the fact that you can "recognize the recognizers," we believe that making recognition a requirement elevates its status to that of a strategic practice. Recognition should be in managers' MBO targets.

A common reply to this concept of having a quota of awards in your MBO plan is, "What if our managers just don't see that much good behavior?" And our response is, "Maybe they should open their eyes. It's almost never because good behavior wasn't there. It just wasn't being noticed and recognized."

In *Reward Systems*, Steve Kerr observes that many "rules" of rewards are actually the cause of dysfunctional reward systems, because they engage in "the folly of rewarding A, while hoping for B."[4] In one common example, he cites the company that wants innovative products and new ideas, but rewards employees who don't make mistakes. The company's reward system is encouraging risk-averse behavior, not innovation (which is inherently risky).

Understand Zero-Value Awards

We all know Facebook's "Like" button. Zero-value awards are similar: people recognize each other with words alone. This is good etiquette, and it offers psychological rewards, but it's not enough to change company culture. Compared to tangible awards, zero-value awards are weak.

Experience reveals the weakness. There are a lot of systems with praise features built in and where there's no budget attached. People are not getting a monetary award, but they're getting a badge on their personal page. This doesn't convey a sense of valuable contribution. I think it's unadvisable to go down this road.

Zero-value awards require little thought. If someone brings refreshments to a meeting, I might consider giving that person a thumbs-up on the system, but will I really take the time for something that trivial? I think an in-person "thanks" is sufficient.

On the other hand, if someone stays up half the night handling a client's crisis, I want to praise this person to the rooftops—I want to demonstrate with the value of my award that what he did really went above and beyond. If I were to just put a badge on his personal page, I'm actually sending the message that extraordinary performance is not much better than bringing refreshments to a meeting. That action is likely to provoke exactly the cynicism I'm working to avoid.

When the system tangibly distinguishes among behaviors, demonstrating that one is somewhat valuable and that another is supervaluable, participation goes up and you get to critical mass. With zero-value awards, people become afraid of offending someone who has worked really hard. You don't want to insult someone with a trivial badge, so you do nothing, and the wisdom-of-crowds effect is lost. In most cases, adoption of this type of recognition program dwindles over time or, worse still, never gets off the ground.

When budgets are attached to rewards, valuable mental judgments are made in relation to every behavior. This reinforces the values and strengthens culture, having an effect on the giver and making the recipient much more emotionally enriched by the reward. The recipient knows it means something!

There is one situation in which zero-value awards add real value, and this is when the community joins in praising an award. The majority of recognition awards go one-to-one or one-to-many. But when it becomes many-to-one, you learn something very powerful about the person receiving the award. It means that there's a multitude of people who feel the same way about that person.

So if I want to give Dan a tangible recognition award for a particular achievement and Cindy beat me to it, I'm not going to put in another award for Dan, because he should receive only one award for that achievement. But I can congratulate Dan on Cindy's award. Others can join in and amplify the praise. Now Dan has the best possible reaction: a tangible award and a chorus of congratulations.

Does Everyone Get an Award?

A common comment in reaction to recognition programs is, "Wait a minute. Not everyone is equally deserving. Not every contestant gets a trophy. If everyone gets an award, don't awards lose meaning?"

That would be true if global social recognition were a zero-sum game, but this confuses the meaning of the recognition experience.

The goal of social recognition is to reinforce certain values and behavior, not to make everyone feel good (the fact that it *does* make people feel good is a benefit, but not the goal).

According to Towers Watson's 2007–2008 Global Workforce study,[5] "Companies with high employee engagement have a 19 percent increase in operating income and almost a 28 percent growth in earnings per share." For a company like Procter & Gamble, this means tens of billions of dollars in additional shareholder value. Engagement won't improve by 15 percent if only 10 percent of the workforce is getting continuous feedback on its performance. Achieving a 90 percent participation rate in a recognition program will cause an increase in engagement in a significant percentage of the workforce. Delivering a 15 percent improvement suddenly looks possible.

In real life, when our clients get to 60 to 80 percent penetration with their recognition programs, a bell curve of award winners appears. The lowest-performing 10 percent of employees will get zero awards, as is appropriate. The middle 80 percent might get two or three awards a year. The top 10 percent will receive perhaps six awards a year.

The people who win ten awards a year are a meritocracy, whatever their position in the company. They are receiving annual awards with an aggregate value of $1,000–$2,000. This is precisely the goal desired in a meritocracy. Top performers will be differentiated whatever their salary bands or whatever the budget for bonuses this year because they lead your culture and the positive business results the culture is designed to deliver.

If only 10 percent of your employees feel like winners, 90 percent feel like losers (a year is a long time to wait for a thank you or even simple feedback on performance). Under such a practice, there is a very small winners' circle. On the other hand, if you've got 90 percent of employees who feel like winners and only 10 percent who feel like losers, that is a much better mix. This draws a much larger and more relevant winners' circle based on merit.

If penetration is high enough, the recognition program becomes self-marketing because the vast majority of employees are winning awards and giving awards. This is the ultimate goal: Employees know about the program, interact with it, redeem awards, and are reminded of the values being promoted by the company. The positive emotional impact from winning recognition ensures that employees are more likely to participate. High participation is inherently efficient. Otherwise, continuous program marketing is necessary, reminding employees it exists, getting them to participate—a death spiral that overtakes too many individual-recognition programs. (Look at it this way: If your benefits were struc-

Can You Give Too Much Recognition?

We understand that setting a target for the number of awards given each week, month, or quarter may be counterintuitive. Sometimes the response is, "Are we just giving everyone a prize? What's the value?" This is a misinterpretation of the weight of awards in a system like this and their place in the HR toolbox.

Remember, strategic recognition does not grant an award to a salesperson who hits his target at the end of the year (that's an incentive). Rather, it grants smaller awards throughout the year whenever he exhibits behavior that is aligned with the company values and objectives. Reinforcing those behaviors helps ensure that he *will* hit his target at the end of the year.

We've heard the objection that managers might give awards that are not deserved, just to hit their target. In our experience, nobody has ever given an excess of recognition. Even if this were to happen, the gap between recognition metrics and department performance will be quickly understood (an underperforming group that gets many, many recognition awards cries out for analysis—another way that metrics create accountability).

Don't underestimate the power of these metrics. Formally establishing a quota of quarterly awards ultimately reminds managers that recognition is actually important in the company. Otherwise, they forget to reward those small, continuous, positive behaviors.

tured so that only 10 percent of employees had them, would the other 90 percent think of benefits as part of their total rewards?)

Recognition and the Marketplace

The third player in all employee-company relationships is the marketplace. Curiously, this is often neglected by managers when they consider the impact of a new practice. Customers, vendors, business partners, shareholders, the media, stakeholders in corporate citizenship, global geographic and online communities that interact with the organization all make up the marketplace that experiences the secondary benefits of social recognition.

Does this seem grandiose? We think not. Let's look at some outcomes of the changes recognition can enable:

- Participation in corporate citizenship, charity work, and community events
- Behaviors and decisions that maximize shareholder value while enacting company values (*double meaning intentional*)
- Cross-cultural information sharing, whether across divisions or around the world

And most importantly:

- Commitment to the customer on behalf of the organization, not just as an individual but also as a representative, indeed—the embodiment—of corporate culture. Jennifer Reimert, vice president of total rewards at Symantec, follows this path when she says, "Employee loyalty drives customer loyalty, which drives revenue, making recognition a business proposition."[6]

Social recognition is a positive player in the talent marketplace. It makes an organization more appealing to job candidates and top talent because they look for an authentic and effective culture. The transparency of today's recruiting means that a company that appreciates its people and maintains high morale and high respect for achievement will have its pick of talent.

Social recognition is regarded positively by the press and opinion leaders, who look both at bottom-line results and management methods. Many companies tried in the 1980s to achieve a Six-Sigma standard; GE did it and received worldwide praise and interest. Companies on

Fortune's 100 Best Companies to Work For list get lots of praise and interest for being on the list (and their return on investment beats that of the competition).

Social recognition, in sum, is a multidimensional practice with positive effects inside and outside the organization. It touches every other company initiative because it is focused on the all-important interplay of group culture and individual needs.

What You Need for Social Recognition

We've seen social recognition work around the world because it is built around the realities of today's corporations and the mindset of today's employees. Almost any recognition program brings benefits, but a program that is planned, launched, and operated as a major management initiative brings competitive advantage in abundance. In a world where most HR tools have been commoditized, why would a business striving to compete do anything less?

As you prepare to design and launch a program of social recognition, review the following checklist of essential building blocks of a truly successful recognition program. Double-check that the following five elements of your program are in place. When they are, you can give a green light to the program launch and bring true social recognition to your organization. (See Figure A.1.)

1. *The stated vision.* Confirm that you have stated the overall, global vision for the program and describe, as metrics or Key Performance Indicators, your program's targets. These can be something like, "Improve employee satisfaction scores from current levels by 15 percent," "Increase employee satisfaction scores around recognition and appreciation by 30 percent," "Achieve employee satisfaction scores related to recognition of 85 percent," "Achieve Q12 scores of X," and so on.

2. *Executive dashboard.* Create an executive dashboard report that uses real data to monitor progress in meeting the targets established. The

report should list the companywide "vision" metrics at the top and the nuts and bolts metrics in graph form underneath (these include overall penetration levels, penetration of each division/department, and operational necessities such as award approval/disapproval levels, enterprise budget targets, etc.). To take this one step further, draft an executive dashboard report with the data you anticipate six months after the recognition program has been launched. When you get to that date, compare the projection with the reality.

3. *Values distribution analysis.* Generate values distribution analysis charts from the data you collect. Executive leaders agree to monitor the data and take corrective action if the results identify any problems. As we've said, social recognition's benefit can lie in revealing which values are lacking as well as which are abundant. It is essential that there is a strong correlation between all awards and company values. If there are some global, all-company, business initiatives (e.g., Six-Sigma), then these can be added to the core values as award areas.

4. *Executive sponsor.* Make sure that there is one or more executive sponsor in place to ensure that the social recognition program delivers what it promises. The executive sponsors will need to agree to monitor and discuss the quarterly executive dashboard and take any corrective action that is needed. Of course, they cannot do this if they have not been empowered by top leadership to do so, and they will not be effective if they do not agree with the targets that have been established. Often the head of HR is one of the executive sponsors, but there should also be someone from another division of the company.

5. *Leader accountability.* At an operational level, program metrics must be broken down into relevant targets for each division/department/country leader or grouping (depending on the company). These leaders could be the people who approve the awards, for example. Without targets, these leaders will not have true accountability for the success of the recognition program. These leaders will have their individual activity metrics communicated to them and will be

accountable for monitoring progress. Ideally, this accountability for the recognition program will be included in the management by objectives plans for these managers. By setting targets for recognition in their departments, reviewing recognition metrics regularly, and tweaking the program as necessary, companies can make the social recognition program become a natural part of the management rhythm.

NOTES

Chapter 1

1. All characters in the dialogues, screenshots, and product examples used in this book are fictional.
2. Anderson, Janna and Lee Rainie, Pew Internet Project, "Millennials Will Benefit and Suffer due to Their Hyperconnected Lives," February 2012.
3. 2010 Study on the State of Performance Management, A report by WorldatWork and Sibson Consulting, October, 2010.
4. Welch, Jack with Suzy Welch, *Winning*, New York, HarperCollins, 2005.
5. DeNisi, Angelo S., and Avraham N. Kluger, "Feedback Effectiveness: Can 360-Degree Appraisals Be Improved?," *The Academy of Management Executive* (1993–2005), Vol. 14, No. 1.
6. Ibid.
7. Welch, Jack with Suzy Welch, *Winning*, New York: HarperCollins, 2005.
8. Eichenwald, Kurt, "How Microsoft Lost Its Mojo," *Vanity Fair*, August, 2012. [Note: this was retitled "Microsoft's Lost Decade" for the web version: http://www.vanityfair .com/business/2012/08/microsoft-lost-mojo-steve-ballmer].

Chapter 2

1. Surowiecki, James, *The Wisdom of Crowds: Why the Many Are Smarter Than the Few and How Collective Wisdom Shapes Business, Economies, Societies and Nations*, New York, Doubleday, 2004.
2. Kickstarter.com is one prominent example of a business whose entire value is mediating between entrepreneurs needing funds and millions of potential investors.
3. IEM__ Iowa Electonic Markets—The University of Iowa. Web. 2012. See http:// tippie.uiowa.edu/iem/.
4. Surowiecki, James, *The Wisdom of Crowds*, New York: Random House, 2005.
5. Ibid.
6. Ibid.
7. Interview with Globoforce, August 2012.
8. Bock, Wally, Three Star Leadership (blog), "Home Depot at 30: A Lesson in Corporate Culture," June 22, 2009 (http://blog.threestarleadership.com/2009/06/22 /home-depot-at-30-a-lesson-in-corporate-culture.aspx), also "Lessons from the Rise and Fall of Delta Airlines, June 16, 2009 (http://blog.threestarleadership .com/2009/06/16/lessons-from-the-rise-and-fall-of-delta-airlines.aspx).

Chapter 3

1. Robinson, Jennifer, "Managing Your Workforce Amid Intense Uncertainty," *Gallup Business Journal*, October 2012.

2. Hsieh, Tony, *Delivering Happiness: A Path to Profits, Passion and Purpose*, New York: Grand Central Publishing, 2013.
3. For the entire list, see http://www.talbenshahar.com/.
4. Gilbert, Daniel, *Stumbling on Happiness*, New York: Knopf, 2006.
5. Amabile, Teresa, and Steven Kramer, "Do Happier People Work Harder?," *The New York Times*, September 3, 2011.
6. Chafkin, Max, "The Zappos Way of Managing," *Inc.* magazine, May 1, 2009, (http://www.inc.com/magazine/20090501/the-zappos-way-of-managing.html).
7. Schumpeter (columnist), "Hating What You Do," *The Economist*, October 6, 2009, http://www.economist.com/businessfinance/displaystory.cfm?story_id=14586131.

Chapter 4

1. Bell, Gordon, and Jim Gemmell, *Your Life, Uploaded* (previously titled *Total Recall*) (New York: Dutton, 2009 and Plume, 2010).
2. Wortham, Jenna, "Meet Memoto, the Lifelogging Camera," *The New York Times* online March 8, 2013.
3. Siedman, Dov, *How: Why HOW We Do Anything Means Everything*, Hoboken NJ: Wiley, 2007.
4. Faragher, Jo, "Productivity and Motivation: Being appreciated delivers bottom-line benefits—Personnel Today's exclusive survey," *Personnel Today*, July 1, 2008: "The unanimous finding of our survey was that appreciative colleagues have a positive effect on productivity: Two-thirds believed they were a lot more productive when given encouragement by their workmates."
5. Gray, Lelia, "Gamers Succeed Where Scientists Fail," University of Washington (http://www.washington.edu/news/2011/09/19/gamers-succeed-where-scientists-fail/) also "Gamification: Experts expect 'game layers' to expand in the future, with positive and negative results," Pew Internet & American Life Project, 2012.
6. Incentive Research Foundation, *2012 Trends in Rewards and Recognition* (report), Available at http://theirf.org/research/content/6085946/2012-trends-in-rewards-recognition/.

Chapter 5

1. Interview with Globoforce, August, 2012.
2. Ibid
3. I'll add that small companies are like towns. The differences are chiefly ones of scale.
4. Interview with Kevin Thompson, senior manager at IBM's Center for Applied Insights.
5. Ferreira Bento, Regina, Lourdes Ferreira White, and Susan Rawson Zacur, "The Stigma of Obesity and Discrimination in Performance Appraisal: A Theoretical Model," *The International Journal of Human Resource Management*, 23 (15), 2012.
6. Pink, Daniel H., *Free Agent Nation: How America's New Independent Workers Are Transforming the Way We Live*. New York: Warner Books, 2001.
7. "Organizational Culture: Talking with the Taxman About Poetry," BlessingWhite, eNews, October 2011.
8. Collins, Jim, and Jerry I. Porras, *Built to Last*, New York, HarperBusiness, 1994; Collins, Jim, *Good to Great*, New York, HarperBusiness, 2001.
9. Schwartz, Tony, The Energy Project, from The Energy Project website: http://www.theenergyproject.com/tools/key-ideas.

10. Gebauer, Julie, and Don Lowman, *Closing the Engagement Gap: How Great Companies Unlock Employee Potential for Superior Results,* New York, Portfolio/Penguin, 2008.
11. The Conference Board, "Employee Engagement in a VUCA (Volatile, Uncertain, Complex, Ambiguous) World," 2011.
12. See citations at http://www.globoforce.com/gfblog/2012/good-and-bad-engagement-all-engagement-is-not-created-equal/.
13. "Employee Engagement: What's Your Engagement Ratio?," Gallup Consulting, 2010.
14. Schwartz, Tony, The Energy Project, from The Energy Project web site: http://www.theenergyproject.com/tools/key-ideas.
15. Strack, Rainer, Jean-Michel Caye, Carsten von der Linden, Horacio Quiros, and Pieter Haen, "From Capability to Profitability: Realizing the Value of People Management," The Boston Consulting Group and World Federation of People Management Associations, July 2012.
16. Interview with Globoforce, July 2012.
17. Numerous studies conclude this; for an example, see The Hay Group study announced at http://www.haygroup.com/ie/press/details.aspx?id=27599.
18. Globoforce Workforce Mood Tracker Survey, Fall 2012.
19. Interview with Globoforce, July 2012.
20. Interview with Globoforce, July 2012.
21. Sibson Consulting and WorldatWork, "2010 Study on the State of Performance Management,"
22. See http://businessjournal.gallup.com/content/124214/driving-engagement-focusing-strengths.aspx.
23. Watson Wyatt Worldwide, 2008/2009 WorkUSA Report
24. Widely quoted. See Forbes online for example: http://www.forbes.com/sites/kevinkruse/2012/10/16/quotes-on-leadership/.
25. Sheridan, Kevin, *Building a Magnetic Culture: How to Attract and Retain Top Talent to Create and Engaged, Productive Workforce.* New York: McGraw-Hill, 2012.

Chapter 6

1. Pulakos, Elaine D., *Performance Management*, Effective Practice Guidelines Report, SHRM Foundation 2004.
2. Interview with Globoforce, December 2012.
3. "Employee Recognition at Intuit," Stanford Graduate School of Business, Case HR-31, March 10, 2008.
4. "Employee Recognition at Intuit," Stanford Graduate School of Business, Case HR-31, March 10, 2008.
5. Interview with Globoforce, July 2012.
6. Holincheck, James, *2012 Strategic Road Map for Employee Performance Management* (report), Gartner, March 2012.
7. Welch, Jack with Suzy Welch, *Winning*, New York, HarperBusiness, 2005. See also http://www.welchway.com/Principles/Differentiation.aspx.
8. *Trends in Employee Recognition 2011*, WorldatWork (report), May 2011. See also http://www.worldatwork.org/waw/adimLink?id=51194)).
9. For the sake of example, I'll assume that bonus is 10 percent of payroll; thus 1 percent of payroll is 10 percent of bonus allocation.
10. Holincheck, James, , *2012 Strategic Road Map for Employee Performance Management* (report), Gartner, March 2012.

11. The net promoter score is described in Fred Reichheld's invaluable books including *The Ultimate Question* (Boston, Harvard Business School Press, 2006).

Chapter 7
1. Pink, Daniel, "Think Tank: Fix the Workplace, Not the Workers," *The Telegraph* (UK), November 6, 2010.
2. http://www.entrepreneur.com/formnet/form/624
3. David Brooks, "How People Change" *The New York Times,* November 26, 2012.

Chapter 8
1. Holincheck, James. *2012 Strategic Road Map for Employee Performance Management.* Gartner (report) March 2012.

Chapter 9
1. Lewis, Michael, *Moneyball: The Art of Winning an Unfair Game*, New York, W.W. Norton & Co., 2004
2. Silver, Nate, *The Signal and the Noise: Why So Many Predictions Fail—But Some Don't*, New York, The Penguin Press, 2012
3. Brooks, David, "The Philosophy of Data," *The New York Times*, February 5, 2013.
4. Silverman, Rachel Emma, "My Colleague, My Paymaster," *The Wall Street Journal*, January 28, 2013.
5. Boyd, E.B. "At IGN, Employees Use A 'Viral Pay' System to Determine Each Others' Bonuses," *Fast Company*, December 16, 2011.

Chapter 10
1. Hartocollis, Anemona, "New York City Ties Doctors' Income to Quality of Care," *The New York Times,* January 11, 2013.

Appendix
1. Boston, Harvard Business School Press, 2008.
2. Miller, Stephen, "Compensation Programs' ROI Highlighted by Study," (article) *Society of Human Resource Management*, May 2006.
3. Sensenig, Kevin J., "Human Potential Untangled," *T+D* magazine, April 2009.
4. Kerr, Steve, *Reward Systems: Does Yours Measure Up?* Boston, Harvard Business School Press, 2008
5. Towers Watson (then Towers Perrin), "Closing the Engagement Gap: A Road Map for Driving Superior Business Performance," 2008.
6. Globoforce Webinar 2009: http://www.globoforce.com/gfblog/2009/symantec-making-the-business-case-for-employee-recognition-in-a-recession/.

INDEX

ABOUT THE AUTHOR

As cofounder and CEO of Globoforce, **Eric Mosley** has been directing the path of Globoforce as the innovator in the employee recognition industry since the company's beginning. His vision to raise recognition from a tactical, unmeasured, and undervalued effort to a global, social, and strategic program with clear measures for performance and success, is now being realized in some of the world's largest and most complex organizations. Eric continues to shape the vision of innovation for the company and the industry.

As a recognized industry leader, Eric has personally advised some of the largest and most admired companies in the world. His insights have been published in such leading publications as *Fast Company, Forbes, Fortune, Harvard Business Review, The Sunday Times,* and *TIME* magazine and he has presented at industry and investment conferences across the world. Eric is also the coauthor of the critically acclaimed book *Winning with a Culture of Recognition,* which was published in October 2010.

Eric brings a wide range of management and technology experience to his role as CEO of Globoforce. Prior to joining Globoforce, he established himself as an accomplished Internet consultant and architect, holding varied management and technology roles in CSK Software, Bull Cara Group, and Logica Aldiscon. He holds a bachelor's degree in electronics, computers, and telecommunications engineering from the University of Dublin, Trinity College.

ABOUT GLOBOFORCE

Eric cofounded Globoforce in 1999 with the goal of reinventing the employee recognition industry for the multicultural, multigenerational global organization of the 21st century. Globoforce has since become one of the world's leading providers of social recognition solutions, redefining how companies understand, manage, and motivate their employees. Innovative companies around the world use Globoforce's cloud-based social recognition software to reveal the true performance and influence of every employee and to strengthen company culture.

By changing the way company leaders think about recognition from a "nice to have" to a critical business methodology for driving productivity, loyalty, and profits, Globoforce is the acknowledged game changer in the industry. A key component of the company's success lies in its realization that the wants and desires of every generation, every culture, and every employee are unique and highly personal. With the industry's largest selection of local languages and local, street-level reward options, Globoforce helps companies overcome geographic and cultural barriers to motivate their workforces and engage employees more fully in the mission, vision, and values of the organization itself. With Globoforce, HR and business leaders can take a strategic approach to recognition programs that result in measurable benefits to the bottom line that are driven by increases in employee engagement, retention, and productivity.

More information on Globoforce, its philosophy of recognition, and its unique approach to recognition is available on the company's website at www.globoforce.com. Globoforce is coheadquartered in Southborough, Massachusetts, and Dublin, Ireland.